ESSENTIAL WORDS AND PHRASES

An Illustrated Guide
to Korean

ESSENTIAL WORDS AND PHRASES

An Illustrated Guide
to Korean

Written by **Chad Meyer**
Illustrated by **Kim Moon-jung**

Seoul Selection

ESSENTIAL WORDS AND PHRASES

An Illustrated Guide
to **Korean**

Written by Chad Meyer
Illustrated by Kim Moon-jung

Published by Seoul Selection
4199 Campus Dr., Suite 550
Irvine, CA 92612, USA
Phone: 949-509-6584, Fax: 949-509-6599
Email: publisher@seoulselection.com
Website: www.seoulselection.com

ISBN: 978-1-62412-013-8

Library of Congress Control Number: 2013948685

An Illustrated Guide to Korean: Essential Words and Phrases developed from a personal interest in learning Korean and a desire to discover what makes Korea so unique. Our goal for the series was to design visually appealing content that is engrossing, entertaining, and unlike anything else that's ever been published. This book provides practical information on all aspects of Korean life from a Westerner's perspective. It's something that businessmen, tourists, and even Korean speakers can learn from.

Keep learning and have fun on your journey!

Chad Meyer and Kim Moon-jung

FOREWORD

Learning Korean is difficult for foreigners, just as learning English is challenging for Koreans, mostly due to the inversion in grammar structures. In 2008, *The Korea Times* invited Chad Meyer and his wife Kim Moon-jung to initiate the *Easy to Learn Korean* series, which has become popular among both foreigners and Koreans. Expatriates can learn core expressions in Korean, and Koreans can learn English expressions about daily life. The authors have faithfully respected the three requirements *The Korea Times* suggested when launching the series: real-life expressions in Korean, highlights on the uniqueness of Korea, and a wealth of supplementary illustrations. The series drew the attention of readers thanks to the warm and colorful illustrations that accompanied words and phrases, allowing readers to learn Korean and English in a fun way. Throughout the past five years, more than 800 articles in the series have been published.

I am proud that the series has been successful beyond my initial expectations. On *The Korea Times* website alone, the series has often been the most-clicked-on post among the 700,000 daily visitors. Now, the series is being published in book form under the title *An Illustrated Guide to Korean: Essential Words and Phrases*. This book is a must-have item for foreigners who want to get the most out of Korean life as well as for Koreans who want to learn key English expressions. The husband-and-wife team should rightfully command appreciation from the Korean government for voluntarily, and unexpectedly, promoting Korea.

Readers of this book won't have to worry about language barriers, as they will be able to express themselves in Korean on the street and at banks, hospitals, markets, tourist sites, subways, and restaurants. Knowing key words and phrases really is enough to help foreigners communicate without difficulty. The bilingualism of the authors has made the high-quality Korean and English expressions found throughout the book possible.

Lee Chang-sup

Chief Editorial Writer / Executive Director
The Korea Times

CONTENTS >>>>>>

CONTENTS ≫≫≫≫

CONTENTS >>>>>>

*A Note Regarding the Korean Romanization Method

The Romanization of all Korean words and sentences that appear in this book is based on the official language standards published by the South Korean Ministry of Culture and Tourism in 2000. We have complied with the standard rules of Korean pronunciation (see Section I-A below). The hyphen (-) is only used in limited situations, namely when 1) *n* and *g* are used as separate consonants as opposed to the *ng* that corresponds to the Korean consonant ㅇ, and 2) several vowels appear in a row, making it difficult to determine the correct pronunciation (see Section III-B below).

A summary of the specific Romanization rules is provided below, along with examples.

Romanization of Korean

I. Basic Principles of Romanization

A. Romanization is based on standard Korean pronunciation.

B. Symbols other than Roman letters are avoided as much as possible.

II. Summary of the Romanization System

A. Vowels are transcribed as follows:

1. Simple Vowels

ㅏ	ㅓ	ㅗ	ㅜ	ㅡ	ㅣ	ㅐ	ㅔ	ㅚ	ㅟ
a	eo	o	u	eu	i	ae	e	oe	wi

2. Diphthongs

ㅑ	ㅕ	ㅛ	ㅠ	ㅒ	ㅖ	ㅘ	ㅙ	ㅝ	ㅞ	ㅢ
ya	yeo	yo	yu	yae	ye	wa	wae	wo	we	ui

Note 1: ㅢ is transcribed as *ui*, even when pronounced as ㅣ.
Note 2: Long vowels are not indicated in Romanization.

B. Consonants are transcribed as follows:

1. Plosives (Stops)

ㄱ	ㄲ	ㅋ	ㄷ	ㄸ	ㅌ	ㅂ	ㅃ	ㅍ
g, k	kk	k	d, t	tt	t	b, p	pp	p

2. Affricates

ㅈ	ㅉ	ㅊ
J	jj	ch

3. Fricatives

ㅅ	ㅆ	ㅎ
s	ss	h

4. Nasals

ㄴ	ㅁ	ㅇ
n	m	ng

5. Liquids

ㄹ
R, l

Note 1: ㄱ, ㄷ, and ㅂ are transcribed as *g*, *d*, and *b* when they appear before a vowel and are transcribed as *k*, *t*, and *p* when followed by another consonant or when appearing at the end of a word.
(Romanization is based on the actual pronunciation, which is enclosed in brackets.)

구미	Gumi	영동	Yeongdong	백암	Baegam
옥천	Okcheon	합덕	Hapdeok	호법	Hobeop
월곶[월곧]	Wolgot	벚꽃[벋꼳]	Beotkkot	한밭[한받]	Hanbat

Note 2: ㄹ is transcribed as *r* when followed by a vowel and as *l* when followed by a consonant or when appearing at the end of a word. ㄹㄹ is transcribed as *ll*

구리	Guri	설악	Seorak	칠곡	Chilgok
임실	Imsil	울릉	Ulleung	대관령[대괄령]	Daegwallyeong

III. Exceptional Cases in Romanization

A. The sounds made by *hangeul* letters are sometimes altered by the letters that surround them. These situations are outlined below, with a guide to the Romanization of the resulting sounds.

1. Assimilation of adjacent consonants

백마[뱅마]	Baengma	신문로[신문노]	Sinmunno	종로[종노]	Jongno
왕십리[왕심니]	Wangsimni	별내[별래]	Byeollae	신라[실라]	Silla

2. Epenthesis (addition of sounds) with ㄴ and ㄹ

학여울[항녀울]	Hangnyeoul	알약[알략]	allyak

3. Palatalization (pronunciation at the palate of the mouth)

해돋이[해도지]	haedoji	같이[가치]	gachi	맞히다[마치다]	machida

4. Aspiration that occurs when ㄱ, ㄷ, ㅂ, and ㅈ appear next to ㅎ

좋고[조코]	joko	놓다[노타]	nota
잡혀[자펴]	japyeo	낳지[나치]	nachi

However, aspirated sounds are not expressed in nouns in which ㅎ follows ㄱ, ㄷ, and ㅂ, as in the examples below.

- 묵호(Mukho) • 집현전(Jiphyeonjeon)

Note: Glottalized (tense) sounds are not shown when they are produced by the combination of separate morphemes, as in the examples below.

압구정	Apgujeong	낙동강	Nakdonggang	죽변	Jukbyeon
낙성대	Nakseongdae	합정	Hapjeong	팔당	Paldang

B. When there is the possibility of confusion in pronunciation, a hyphen (-) may be used.

중앙	Jung-ang	반구대	Ban-gudae
세운	Se-un	해운대	Hae-undae

C. The first letter of proper names is capitalized.

부산	Busan	세종	Sejong

D. Personal names are written with the family name first, followed by a space and the given name. The syllables of the given name are written without a space between them, but it is acceptable to separate them with a hyphen (see parentheses).

- 민용하 Min Yongha (Min Yong-ha)   • 송나리 Song Nari (Song Na-ri)

1. Assimilated sound changes that occur between syllables in given names are not reflected in Romanization.

2. These rules do not govern the Romanization of family names.

E. Administrative units such as 도, 시, 군, 구, 읍, 면, 리, 동, and 가 are Romanized as *do*, *si*, *gun*, *gu*, *eup*, *myeon*, *ri*, *dong*, and *ga*, and a hyphen is placed between them and the preceding place name. Assimilated sound changes occurring between the place name and the administrative unit are not reflected in the Romanization.

F. Names of geographic features, cultural properties, and man-made structures that include an explanatory suffix such as 산, 강, 궁, and so on are written as a single word. In such words, a hyphen is not used to separate the proper noun from the explanatory suffix.

남산	Namsan	속리산	Songnisan	금강	Geumgang
독도	Dokdo	경복궁	Gyeongbokgung	무량수전	Muryangsujeon

G. Proper names such as the names of people, companies, and organizations may continue to be written as they have been in the past.

H. In academic articles and other special cases where the reader may have to convert the Romanized Korean back into *hangeul* at some later point, the text is Romanized according to the actual *hangeul* spelling, not according to its pronunciation. In such cases, each *hangeul* letter is Romanized as explained in Section II except for ㄱ, ㄷ, ㅂ, and ㄹ, which are always written as *g*, *d*, *b*, and *l*. When ㅇ has no sound value, it is replaced by a hyphen. A hyphen may also be used when it is necessary to distinguish between syllables.

집	jib	짚	jip	밖	bakk
굳이	gud-i	좋다	johda	가곡	gagog
조랑말	jolangmal	없었습니다.	eobs-eoss-seubnida		

Note: The material in this section was based on the explanation of the Romanization of Korean that is provided, along with information about other language standards, by the National Institute of the Korean Language.

ESSENTIAL
EXPRESSIONS

1 ESSENTIAL EXPRESSIONS

FIRST MEETINGS & INTRODUCTIONS

first meetings

첫 만남
cheot mannam

> **Hello.**
> 안녕하세요.
> *annyeonghaseyo.*

Hello.
○ 안녕하세요.
annyeonghaseyo.

I'm _____.
○ 저는 _____라고 합니다.
jeo-neun _____ rago hamnida.

My name is _____.
○ 제 이름은 _____입니다.
je ireumeun _____imnida.

How do you do?

처음 뵙겠습니다.
cheo-eum boepgetseumnida.

The literal meaning is "This is [my] first time meeting you."

introductions

자기소개
jagisogae

Pleased to meet you.

만나서 반갑습니다.
mannaseo ban-gapseumnida.

Pleased to meet you.

만나서 반갑습니다.
mannaseo ban-gapseumnida.

Pleased to meet you, too.

저도 만나서 반갑습니다.
jeodo mannaseo ban-gapseumnida.

I hope we get along well together.

앞으로 잘 부탁드립니다.
apeuro jal butakdeurimnida.

EVERYDAY GREETINGS

greetings

인사

insa

Good morning.

좋은 아침이에요.

jo-eun achimieyo!

Good morning.

안녕하세요?

annyeonghaseyo?

Good morning. / Good afternoon. / Good evening. / Hello. / Hi.

○ 안녕하십니까? (formal)

annyeonghasimnikka?

○ 안녕하세요? (polite common)

annyeonghaseyo?

○ 안녕! (informal, used among close friends)

annyeong!

These three greetings are identical in meaning and can be used at any time of day. As is common in Korean, a statement and response can use the same wording. 안녕하세요 and 안녕 can each be used as a statement and also as a response. It's important to maintain the politeness level in conversation. Be sure to use the appropriate politeness level for the person you are talking to.

Good morning.

좋은 아침이에요.
jo-eun achimieyo!

It's been a long time since we last met!

오래간만이네요!
oraeganmanineyo!

How are you?

잘 지내셨어요?
jal jinaesyeosseoyo?

How have you been?

요즘, 어떻게 지내세요?
yojeum, eotteoke jinaeseyo?

I'm doing well.

잘 지내요 / 좋아요.
jal jinaeyo / joayo.

I have been really busy.

정말 바빴어요.
jeongmal bappasseoyo.

You look good.

좋아 보이네요.
joa boineyo.

It was a pleasure meeting you.

만나서 반가웠어요.
mannaseo bangawosseoyo.

Well, I look forward to seeing you again.

◌ 그럼, 또 뵙겠습니다. (formal)
geureom, tto boepgetseumnida.

◌ 그럼, 또 만나요! (polite common)
geureom, tto mannayo!

Take care. / Good-bye.

◌ 잘 가요.
Jal gayo.

Good-bye. (speaker is leaving, others stay)

◌ 안녕히 계세요.
annyeonghi gyeseyo.

Good-bye. (speaker is staying while others leave, or everyone leaves together)

◌ 안녕히 가세요.
annyeonghi gaseyo.

Saying good-bye in Korean requires identifying who is staying and who is leaving. The expressions above mean "stay in peace" (*annyeonghi gyeseyo*) or "go in peace" (*annyeonghi gaseyo*).

If the speaker is leaving while the other people remain, he would say *annyeonghi gyeseyo*. However, if the speaker stays and the others leave, then he would say *annyeonghi gaseyo*. If all parties are leaving simultaneously, everyone will say *annyeonghi gaseyo*.

farewells

작별인사
jakbyeorinsa

Good bye.
안녕히 가세요
annyeonghi gaseyo.

Good bye!
안녕히 계세요.
annyeonghi gyeseyo.

Good night.

○ 안녕히 주무세요. (formal)
annyeonghi jumuseyo.

○ 잘 자요. (polite common)
jal jayo.

Sweet dreams.

○ 좋은 꿈꾸세요.
jo-eun kkumkkuseyo.

GRATITUDE & APOLOGIES

Thank you.
감사합니다.
gamsahamnida.

gratitude
감사
gamsa

I'm sorry.
죄송합니다.
joesonghamnida.

apologies
사과
sagwa

Thank you.

 감사합니다. (formal)
gamsahamnida.

○ 고마워요. (polite common)
gomawoyo.

○ 고마워. (informal)
gomawo.

You're welcome.

○ 천만에요.
cheonmaneyo.

Don't mention it.

별 말씀을요.

byeol malsseumeuryo.

You've been a really big help.

정말 큰 도움을 받았습니다.

jeongmal keun doumeul badatseumnida.

It's my pleasure (to help).

도움이 되었다니 기쁩니다.

doumi doe-eotdani gippeumnida.

I'm sorry.

죄송합니다. (formal)

joesonghamnida.

미안해요. (polite common)

mianhaeyo.

Don't worry about it.

괜찮습니다. 걱정마십시오.

gwaenchansseumnida. geokjeonghajimasipsio.

It's no problem. / It's all right. / It's okay.

괜찮아요.

gwaenchanayo

Excuse me.

실례합니다.

sillyehamnida.

OK, that's good!
네. 좋아요!
ne, joayo!

That's not possible.
그건 좀 곤란한데요.
geugeon jom gollanhandeyo.

saying yes
승낙
seungnak

saying no
거절
geojeol

Okay! / That's good!
○ 네. 좋아요!
ne, joayo!

That's great!
○ 정말 좋은데요.
jeongmal jo-eundeyo.

Great idea! Let's do it.
○ 좋아요! 그렇게 해요.
joayo! geureoke haeyo.

I'm not sure about that.

글쎄요. 잘 모르겠는데요.
geulsseyo. jal moreugenneundeyo.

No.

아니요.
aniyo.

No, thank you.

아닙니다, 괜찮습니다.
animnida, gwaenchansseumnida.

Thank you, but I'd rather not.

고맙지만 사양하겠습니다.
gomapjiman sayanghagetseumnida.

That's not possible.

그건 좀 곤란한데요.
geugeon jom gollanhandeyo.

I really don't want to. / I won't do it. / I hate (that).

전 싫어요.
jeon sireoyo.

In Korea, people speak in an indirect manner to be polite. If you need to say "no" or reject something, always do so in the politest way possible. It's rude to simply say "no."

COMPREHENSION & ASKING AGAIN

confusion

혼동
hondong

I don't understand.
이해를 못했어요.
ihaereul motaesseoyo.

I only speak a little Korean.
한국어 조금 밖에 못해요.
han-gugeo jogeum bakke motaeyo.

Can you speak more slowly?
좀 천천히 얘기해 주시겠어요?
jom cheoncheonhi yaegihae jusigesseoyo?

I'm sorry, but I don't understand.
죄송해요. 무슨 말인지 이해를 못했어요.
joesonghaeyo. museun marinji ihaereul motaesseoyo.

Could you please say that again?
다시 한 번만 말씀해 주세요.
dasi han beonman malsseumhae juseyo.

> **Ah, now I get it.**
> 아, 이제 알겠어요.
> *a, ije algesseoyo.*

Could you please repeat the question?
질문을 다시 말씀해 주시겠어요?
jilmuneul dasi malsseumhae jusigesseoyo?

Ah, now I get it. / Ah, now I understand.
아, 이제 알겠어요.
a, ije algesseoyo.

I understand.
이해해요.
ihaehaeyo.

You are very good at Korean.
한국어 참 잘하시네요.
han-gugeo cham jalhasineyo.

I'm studying Korean.
한국어를 공부하고 있어요.
han-gugeoreul gongbuhago isseoyo.

FEELINGS

I'm happy.

(나는) **기분이 좋아요.**

(na-neun) gibuni joayo.

I'm angry.

(나는) **화났어요.**

(na-neun) hwanasseoyo.

I'm excited.

(나는) **신나요.**

(na-neun) sinnayo.

I'm bored.

(나는) **지루해요.**

(na-neun) jiruhaeyo.

I'm sick.

(나는) **아파요.**

(na-neun) apayo.

I'm sad.

(나는) **슬퍼요.**

(na-neun) seulpeoyo.

I'm hungry.

(나는) **배가 고파요.**

(na-neun) baega gopayo.

I'm thirsty.

(나는) **목이 말라요.**

(na-neun) mogi mallayo.

I'm tired.

(나는) **피곤해요.**

(na-neun) pigonhaeyo.

I'm disappointed.

(나는) **실망했어요.**

(na-neun) silmanghaesseoyo.

The personal pronoun *na*, meaning "I," is not required in Korean as it is in English. However, if you want to emphasize something about yourself, you can add the *neun* subject marker after "I": *na-neun* or *jeo-neun* (*jeo* is a more polite version of *na*). This is noted with the optional *na-neun* in parentheses in the pictures above.

TALKING ON THE PHONE

telephone conversation

전화 대화

jeonhwa daehwa

> **Hello?**
> 여보세요?
> *yeoboseyo?*

Hello?

○ 여보세요?
yeoboseyo?

Is this _____?

○ 거기 _____, 맞나요?
geogi _____, mannayo?

Yes, it is.

○ 네, 그런데요.
ne, geureondeyo.

This is _____ . May I speak to _____?

○ 저는 _____라고 하는데요. _____ 좀 바꿔주시겠어요?
jeo-neun _____rago haneundeyo. _____ jom bakkwojusigesseoyo?

Yes, this is he / she.

○ 네, 접니다.
ne, jeomnida.

Please wait a minute. I'll get him / her.

○ 잠깐만 기다리세요. 바꿔드릴게요.
jamkkanman gidariseyo. bakkwodeurilgeyo.

_____, you have a phone call.

○ _____씨, 전화 왔어요.
_____ssi, jeonhwa wasseoyo.

This is _____.

○ 네, 전화 바꿨습니다.
ne, jeonhwa bakkwotseumnida.

The line is busy.

○ 통화 중이세요.
tonghwa jung-iseyo.

He's not here right now.

○ 지금 안 계신데요.
jigeum an gyesindeyo.

He will be back around 7 pm.

○ 오후 7시에 돌아오시는데요.
ohu ilgopsie doraosi-neundeyo.

Could I leave a message?

○ 그럼 말씀 좀 전해 주시겠어요?
geureom malsseum jom jeonhae jusigesseoyo?

Could you please tell him that I called?

⟳ 제가 전화했었다고 전해주시겠어요?
jega jeonhwahaesseotdago jeonhaejusigesseoyo?

May I ask who's calling?

⟳ 실례지만 누구십니까?
sillyejiman nugusimnikka?

My name is _____ and my number is _____.

⟳ 제 이름은 _____고, 제 전화번호는 _____입니다.
je ireumeun _____ go, je jeonhwabeonho-neun _____ imnida.

I'll give her / him your message as soon as she / he returns.

⟳ 들어오시는 대로 말씀 전하겠습니다.
deureo-osi-neun daero malsseum jeonhagetseumnida.

SMALL TALK AND
MAKING FRIENDS

2 SMALL TALK AND MAKING FRIENDS

OVERVIEW Tenses

Like English, Korean has three basic tenses: past, present, and future.

The present tense is used to describe a fact, something that is unchanging or something that you always do.

The basic form is: (Verb root) + -아요 or -어요.

Examples:

먹다 (to eat) Root: 먹–	**Present:** 먹어요. I eat.
가다 (to go) Root: 가–	**Present:** 가요. I go.

Note:
-Use -아요 if the last vowel of the root is ㅗ or ㅏ.
-Otherwise, use -어요.

The past tense is used to describe events that have already occurred and are complete.

The form is: (Root) + -었어요 or (Root) + -았어요.

먹다 (to eat) Root: 먹–	**Past:** 먹었어요. I ate.
가다 (to go) Root: 가–	**Past:** 갔어요. I went.

Note:
-Use -았어요 if the last vowel of the root is ㅗ or ㅏ.
-Otherwise, use -었어요.

The future tense is used to describe something that will probably happen but hasn't yet started.

> **The form is: (Root) + (으)ㄹ 거예요.**

| 먹다 (to eat) Root: 먹– | **Future:** 먹을 거예요. I will eat. |
| 가다 (to go) Root: 가– | **Future:** 갈 거예요. I will go. |

Note:
-Use –을 거예요 if the root ends in a consonant.
-Use –ㄹ 거예요 if the root ends in a vowel.

The progressive aspect is used to describe something that has started but hasn't been completed (similar to the –ing in "running," "eating," "sleeping," etc.). As with English, the progressive tense is often used while speaking.

> **The form is: (Root) + 고 있어요.**

먹다 (to eat) Root: 먹–

Present progressive: 먹고 있어요. I'm eating.

가다 (to go) Root: 가–

Present progessive: 가고 있어요. I'm going.

These are the basic rules for regular verbs. There are also irregular verbs that take slightly different forms.

This may be intimidating to beginners, but you will get used to it with practice. Make sure you understand the basics, and if possible, practice speaking with Koreans as much as possible.

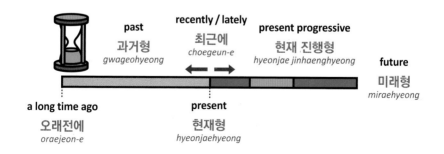

past
과거형
gwageohyeong

recently / lately
최근에
choegeun-e

present progressive
현재 진행형
hyeonjae jinhaenghyeong

future
미래형
miraehyeong

a long time ago
오래전에
oraejeon-e

present
현재형
hyeonjaehyeong

name

이름
ireum

May I have your name?

◌ 성함이 어떻게 되세요?
seonghami eotteoke doeseyo?

What's your name?

◌ 이름이 뭐예요?
ireumi mwo-yeyo?

When you meet someone older than you, a customer, or a senior co-worker, you should ask for their name with the formal polite *seonghami eotteoke doeseyo?* The expression *ireumi mwo-yeyo* is the polite common form and can only be used with people who are the same age, younger, or lower in company rank.

My name is _____.

○ 제 이름은 _____입니다.
je ireumeun _____imnida.

I'm _____.

○ 저는 _____라고 합니다.
jeo-neun _____rago hamnida.

nationality

국적
gukjeok

Where are you from?

○ 어느 나라에서 오셨어요?
eoneu nara-eseo osyeosseoyo?

I'm from the US.

○ 미국에서 왔습니다.
migugeseo watseumnida.

What's your nationality?

○ 어느 나라 사람이에요?
eoneu nara saramieyo?

Eoneu nara-eseo osyeosseoyo? literally means, "Which country did you come from?" *Eoneu nara saramieyo?* has the same meaning but literally translates to as, "Which country's person are you?"

I'm British.

○ 전 영국인이에요.
jeon yeongguk-inieyo.

Is this your first time in Korea?

○ 한국에 이번이 처음이세요?
han-guge ibeoni cheo-eumiseyo?

This is my second time here.

○ 이번이 두 번째입니다.
ibeoni du beonjjae-imnida.

What brought you here?

○ 무슨 일로 여기 오셨어요?
museun illo yeogi osyeosseoyo?

I'm on vacation.

○ 휴가로 왔습니다.
hyugaro watseumnida.

How long have you been in Korea?

○ 한국에 계신 지 얼마나 되셨어요?
han-guge gyesin ji eolmana doesyeosseoyo?

I've been in Korea for two years.

○ 한국에 온 지 2년 됐습니다.
han-guge on ji inyeon dwaetseumnida.

age

나이

nai

unmarried woman / young lady	unmarried man / young man	married woman	married man
아가씨	**총각**	**아줌마 / 아주머니**	**아저씨**
agassi	*chonggak*	*ajumma / ajumeoni*	*ajeossi*

How old are you?

나이가 어떻게 되세요?
naiga eotteoke doeseyo?

I'm _____ years old.

저는 _____살입니다.
jeo-neun _____salimnida.

Koreans consider themselves to be age one at birth. When giving ages, they use pure Korean numbers (*hana, dul, set*) not the Sino-Korean numbers (*il, i, sam*). Koreans address older friends and older siblings with respectful titles. Instead of that person's given name, people are addressed using terms such as *eonni* (older sister) and *oppa* (older brother) by women and *nuna* (older sister) and *hyeong* (older brother) by men.

I'm younger (than you).

○ 제가 어리네요
jega eorineyo.

I'm a lot older (than you).

○ 제가 나이가 많네요.
jega naiga manneyo.

You look young for your age.

○ 나이보다 젊어 보이세요.
naiboda jeolmeo boiseyo.

You have a baby face.

○ 동안이세요.
dong-aniseyo.

---

*A*jumma, *ajumeoni*, and *ajeossi* are terms to describe people who are married or of marrying age. As a beginner, it's best to avoid using these terms, as people may take offense to being called "old." If you want to get someone's attention, try using the polite common-form expression 저기요 (*jeogiyo*), which literally translates to "Hey there."

Another tip: a woman of *ajumma* age will be thrilled if you call her *agassi* or comment on her youthful-looking face (*dong-an*).

Did you come to Korea by yourself?

○ 한국에는 혼자 오셨나요?
han-guge-neun honja osyeonnayo?

---

family

가족
gajok

Does everyone in your family live in _____ ?

○ 가족들은 다 _____에서 살고 계신 건가요?
gajokdeureun da _____ eseo salgo gyesin geon-gayo?

- -

How many siblings do you have?

○ 형제가 어떻게 되세요?
hyeongjega eotteoke doeseyo?

- -

I have an older brother and an older sister.

○ 오빠 한 명, 언니 한 명이 있습니다. (said by female)
oppa han myeong, eonni han myeong-i itseumnida.

○ 형 한 명, 누나 한 명이 있습니다. (said by male)
hyeong han myeong, nuna han myeong-i itseumnida.

- -

I'm the middle child of three boys.

우리는 아들만 삼형제인데, 제가 중간이에요.
uri-neun adeulman samhyeongjeinde, jega jungganieyo.

I'm the youngest of three girls.

우리는 딸만 세 자매고, 제가 막내예요.
uri-neun ttalman se jamaego, jega mangnaeyeyo.

I'm an only child.

전 외동이에요.
jeon oedong-ieyo.

May I ask if you're married?

실례지만 결혼하셨어요?
sillyejiman gyeolhonhasyeosseoyo?

No, I'm single.

아니요, 저는 아직 미혼이에요.
aniyo, jeo-neun ajik mihonieyo.

Yes, I'm married and live with my wife in Seoul.

예, 결혼했어요. 지금 아내와 함께 서울에서 살고 있어요.
ye, gyeolhonhaesseoyo. jigeum anaewa hamkke seouleseo salgo isseoyo.

Where are you from?

고향이 어디세요?
gohyang-i eodiseyo?

I'm from Busan.

저는 고향이 부산이에요.
jeo-neun gohyang-i busanieyo.

hometown

고향
gohyang

Where are you from?
고향이 어디세요?
gohyang-i eodiseyo?

Do you still have family in your hometown?

○ 가족들이 아직도 고향에서 살고 계세요?
gajokdeuri ajikdo gohyang-eseo salgo gyeseyo?

What is Busan famous for?

○ 부산은 뭐가 유명한가요?
Busan-eun mwo-ga yumyeonghan-gayo?

My hometown is famous for _____ .

○ 우리 고향은 _____으로 유명해요.
uri gohyang-eun _____ -euro yumyeonghaeyo.

SMALL TALK

asking how people are
안부 묻기
anbu mutgi

You look tired.
피곤해 보이네요.
pigonhae boineyo.

Did you get a good night's sleep?
밤에 잘 주무셨어요?
bam-e jal jumusyeosseoyo?

I slept like a log.
세상 모르고 잤어요.
sesang moreugo jasseoyo.

You look tired.
피곤해 보이네요.
pigonhae boineyo.

I have a lot of stress.
스트레스를 좀 받았어요.
seuteureseureul jom badasseoyo.

weather

날씨
nalssi

The weather's great today.

오늘 날씨가 좋네요.
oneul nalssiga jonneyo.

Yes, it's a sunny day. Do you have any special plans?

그러게요. 날이 참 맑네요. 뭐 좋은 계획 있으세요?
geureogeyo. nari cham mangneyo. mwo jo-eun gyehoek isseuseyo?

It's raining.

비가 오네요.
biga oneyo.

It's cloudy.

날씨가 흐려요.
nalssiga heuryeoyo.

Korea has four distinct seasons, spring and fall being the most comfortable. The rainy season extends from June through July. Expect 80 to 90 percent humidity toward the end of this period.

hobby

취미
chwimi

What are your hobbies?

○ 취미는 무엇입니까?
chwimi-neun mueosimnikka?

I love listening to music.

○ 음악 듣는 것을 정말 좋아해요.
eumak deunneun geoseul jeongmal joahaeyo.

What type of music do you like?

○ 어떤 음악을 좋아하세요?
eotteon eumageul joahaseyo?

Recently, I've been visiting Seoul's museums and art galleries
when I have the time.

○ 저는 요즘 시간 날 때마다 서울의 박물관과 미술관을 찾아다녀요.
*jeo-neun yojeum sigan nal ttaemada seourui bangmulgwan-gwa misulgwaneul
chajadanyeoyo.*

I've been a baseball fan since I was a kid.

저는 어렸을 때부터 야구광이었어요.

jeo-neun eoryeosseul ttaebuteo yagugwang-ieosseoyo.

What's your favorite Korean baseball team?

어느 한국 야구팀을 가장 좋아하세요?

eoneu han-guk yagutimeul gajang joahaseyo?

I'm a fan of the Seoul Heroes.

저는 서울 히어로즈 팬이에요.

jeo-neun seoul hieorojeu paenieyo.

What types of television shows do you like?

어떤 종류의 티브이 프로그램을 좋아하나요?

eotteon jongnyu-ui tibeu-i peurogeuraemeul joahanayo?

These days I'm crazy about Korean soap operas.

저는 요즘에 한국 드라마에 푹 빠졌어요.

jeo-neun yojeume han-guk deurama-e puk ppajyeosseoyo.

I watch the news every night.

저는 매일 저녁 뉴스를 봐요.

jeo-neun maeil jeonyeok nyuseureul bwayo.

Nice talking to you.

얘기 즐거웠어요.

yaegi jeulgeowosseoyo.

The three major tv networks are MBC, SBS, and KBS. KBS is the largest of the three and is funded by the Korean government. Arirang TV is another government-funded station and airs entirely in English.

MAKING PLANS

invitation

초대
chodae

Welcome to my home!
어서 오세요!
eoseo oseyo!

Do you have some free time tonight?

○ 오늘 저녁에 시간 있어요?
oneul jeonyeoge sigan isseoyo?

Yes. Why?

○ 네. 왜요?
ne. waeyo?

Would you like to come over for dinner?

○ 저녁에 저희 집에 식사하러 오시겠어요?
jeonyeoge jeohui jibe siksahareo osigesseoyo?

Thank you, that would be great!

○ 감사합니다, 그러면 저는 너무 좋죠!
gamsahamnida, geureomyeon jeo-neun neomu jochyo!

Welcome to my home!

○ 어서 오세요!

eoseo oseyo!

Thank you for inviting me / us.

○ 초대해 주셔서 감사합니다.

chodaehae jusyeoseo gamsahamnida.

When visiting someone's house for the first time, guests typically bring practical things such as tissue, toilet paper, fruit, or detergent. And remember to take off your shoes before entering the host's house!

Do you have any plans this weekend?

○ 이번 주말에 계획이 어떻게 돼요?

ibeon jumare gyehoegi eotteoke dwaeyo?

Nothing special.

○ 특별한 거 없는데요.

teukbyeolhan geo eomneundeyo.

Why don't we hike Mt. Seoraksan this weekend?

○ 그럼, 이번 주말에 설악산에 등산 가는 거 어때요?

geureom, ibeon jumare seoraksane deungsan ganeun geo eottaeyo?

Do you like watching movies?

○ 영화 보는 거 좋아해요?

yeonghwa boneun geo joahaeyo?

Yes. I do (like it).

○ 네, 좋아해요.
ne, joahaeyo.

Why don't we watch a movie together this weekend?

○ 그럼, 주말에 같이 영화 보는 거 어때요?
geureom, jumare gachi yeonghwa boneun geo eottaeyo?

Yes, that sounds good. When and where should we meet?

○ 좋아요. 그럼, 몇 시, 어디에서 만날까요?
joayo. geureom, myeot si, eodieseo mannalkkayo?

Let's meet at 3 o'clock on Saturday in front of the Daehan Theater near Chungmuro Subway Station.

○ 토요일, 충무로역 대한극장 앞에서 세 시에 만나요.
toyoil, chungmuro-yeok daehan-geukjang apeseo se sie mannayo.

Would you like to have dinner together tonight?

○ 오늘 저녁이나 같이 먹을래요?
oneul jeonyeogina gachi meogeullaeyo?

I'm sorry, I already have plans.

○ 미안해요, 오늘은 선약이 있어요.
mianhaeyo, oneureun seonyagi isseoyo.

I'm sorry, I've got a lot of work today.

○ 미안해요, 오늘은 일이 너무 많아요.
mianhaeyo, oneureun iri neomu manayo.

Not tonight, but how about another day?

○ 오늘 말고 다른 날은 안될까요?
oneul malgo dareun nareun andoelkkayo?

When would be good?

◌ 그럼, 언제가 좋아요?
geureom, eonjega joayo?

getting together for drinks

술약속

suryaksok

Let's have dinner and drinks together soon.

◌ 우리 언제 저녁이나 술 한잔 같이해요.
uri eonje jeonyeogina sul hanjan gachihaeyo.

Sounds great! What about this Friday night?

◌ 좋아요! 이번 주 금요일 밤 어때요?
joayo! ibeon ju geumyoil bam eottaeyo?

Yeah! I know a place that's famous for its *makgeolli* and kimchi pancakes.

◌ 좋죠! 저 막걸리랑 김치전 맛있는 곳 알아요.
jochyo! jeo makgeollirang gimchijeon masinneun got arayo.

COUNTRIES & NATIONALITIES

USA / American
미국 / 미국인
miguk / miguk-in

United Kingdom / British
영국 / 영국인
yeongguk / yeongguk-in

Canada / Canadian
캐나다 / 캐나다인
kaenada / kaenada-in

Australia / Australian
호주 / 호주인
hoju / hoju-in

Japan / Japanese
일본 / 일본인
ilbon / ilbon-in

China / Chinese
중국 / 중국인
jungguk / jungguk-in

India / Indian
인도 / 인도인
indo / indo-in

Singapore / Singaporean
싱가포르 / 싱가포르인
singgaporeu / singgaporeu-in

Germany / German
독일 / 독일인
dogil / dogil-in

France / French

프랑스 / 프랑스인
peurangseu / peurangseu-in

Spain / Spanish

스페인 / 스페인인
seupein / seupein-in

Russia / Russian

러시아 / 러시아인
reosia / reosia-in

Korea / Korean

한국 / 한국인
hanguk / hanguk-in

I'm from Korea.

한국에서 왔어요.
han-gugeseo wasseoyo.

I'm Korean.

전 한국인이에요.
jeon han-guk-inieyo.

FAMILY

maternal grandfather
외할아버지
oe-harabeoji

maternal grandmother
외할머니
oe-halmeoni

paternal grandfather
친할아버지
chin-harabeoji

paternal grandmother
친할머니
chin-halmeoni

mother / mom
어머니 / 엄마
eomeoni / eomma

father / dad
아버지 / 아빠
abeoji / appa

older sister
누나
nuna
(said by male)

언니
eonni
(said by female)

older brother
형
hyeong
(said by male)

오빠
oppa
(said by female)

I / Me
저 (polite) /
나 (informal)
jeo / na

younger sister
여동생
yeo-dongsaeng

younger brother
남동생
nam-dongseang

Younger family members must address older family members respectfully by using their title, as indicated in the diagram above. The proper word for "older brother" or "older sister" will depend on the gender of the younger sibling. If the younger sibling is female, she will call her older sister *eonni*. If the younger sibling is male, he will call his older sister *nuna*.

father-in-law
시아버지
si-abeoji

mother-in-law
시어머니
si-eomeoni

mother-in-law
장모
jangmo

father-in-law
장인
jang-in

daughter-in-law
며느리
myeoneuri

husband
남편
nampyeon

wife
아내
anae

son-in-law
사위
sawi

aunt (mother´s sister) 이모 *imo*
uncle (husband of mother´s sister) 이모부 *imobu*

aunt (father´s sister) 고모 *gomo*
uncle (husband of father's sister) 고모부 *gomobu*

uncle (father´s older brother) 큰아버지 *keunabeoji*
aunt (wife of father´s older brother) 큰어머니 *keuneomeoni*

uncle (father´s younger married brother) 작은아버지 *jageunabeoji*
aunt (wife of father´s younger brother) 작은어머니 *jageuneomeoni*

Younger unmarried uncles from the father's family are known as *samchon*. On the mother's side of the family, *oe-samchon* can be used for any older or younger uncle.

SLANG & COLLOQUIALISMS

You might not experience language problems while learning Korean at the basic level. However, the deeper you get into the language the more you'll realize that slang and colloquialisms are quite common—and challenging. Now is a good time to begin to prepare for how Koreans actually speak.

SLANG

That's awesome!
짱이에요!
jjang-ieyo!

Literal translation: "You are the boss!"

I totally recommend it.
강추합니다.
gangchuhamnida.

Literal translation: "I strongly recommend it."

It's the best.
완전 좋아요.
wanjeon joayo.

Literal translation: "I like it completely."

That sucks. / You are pathetic.
안습이에요.
anseup-ieyo.

Literal translation: "It makes my eyes damp."

That's cool.
죽이네요.
jugineyo.

Literal translation: "It's killing me."

I can't live without it.
완소예요.
wansoyeyo.

Literal translation: "My precious."

Of course.
당근이지.
danggeuniji.

Literal translation: "It's a carrot!" (This is a pun on the similar-sounding "당연하지.")

So embarrassing!
쪽팔리다.
jjokpallida.

Literal translation: "to lose face"

SLANG & COLLOQUIALISMS

You can't be serious.

○ 웃기지마.
utgijima.

- -

Literal translation: "Don't make me laugh."

I'm thrilled with it.

○ 꿀맛 같다.
kkulmat gatda.

- -

Literal translation: "It tastes like honey."

COLLOQUIALISMS

I'm so happy!

○ 날아갈 것 같아요!
naragal geot gatayo!

- -

Literal translation: "I'm flying high right now!"

I'm too busy.

○ 바빠 죽겠어요.
bappa jukgesseoyo.

- -

Literal translation: "I'm so busy I'm dying."

That's absurd.

정말 웃기지도 않아요.
jeongmal utgijido anayo.

Literal translation: "That's not even funny."

I'm going crazy.

미치겠어요.
michigesseoyo.

Literal translation: "I'm going crazy."

I've got problems of my own.

내 코가 석자예요.
nae koga seokjayeyo.

Literal translation: "My runny nose is three feet long."

Time flies.

시간은 화살과 같다.
siganeun hwasalgwa gatda.

Literal translation: "Time is like an arrow."

It's a pie in the sky.

그건 그림의 떡이에요.
geugeon geurimui tteogieyo.

Literal translation: "It's the rice cake in the picture."

SLANG & COLLOQUIALISMS

The grass is always greener on the other side.

◌ 남의 떡이 더 커 보인다.
namui tteogi deo keo boinda.

Literal translation: "The other person's rice cake looks bigger (than mine)."

Actions speak louder than words.

◌ 백 마디 말보다 한 번의 행동이 중요하다.
baek madi malboda han beonui haengdong-i jungyohada.

Literal translation: "One action matters more than 100 words."

No one is perfect.

◌ 원숭이도 나무에서 떨어진다.
wonsung-ido namueseo tteoreojinda.

Literal translation: "Even monkeys fall from trees."

Speak of the devil.

◌ 호랑이도 제 말하면 온다.
horang-ido je malhamyeon onda.

Literal translation: "The tiger will come if you speak of him."

ASKING FOR DIRECTIONS & USING PUBLIC TRANSPORTATION

3 ASKING FOR DIRECTIONS & USING PUBLIC TRANSPORTATION

OVERVIEW Public Transportation System

South Korea has one of those most inexpensive and efficient public transportation systems in the world.

As of 2011, 49 percent of Korea's population lives in or near Seoul, so you can imagine how important infrastructure is. The Seoul public transportation system includes 19 subway lines, four types of public buses, two types of taxis, and an Airport Limousine Bus service.

This may seem like a lot, but by familiarizing yourself with them you can travel anywhere in the country quickly and affordably.

subway

지하철
jihacheol

As of 2013, the greater Seoul area has 19 metropolitan subway lines, with surface lines connecting to them from the state-run Korean National Railroad (KORAIL). These subway lines link Seoul to satellite cites, with numerous transfer stations along the way.

Seoul's subway is easy to use and inexpensive. Most platform and train signs are in English and Korean. There is also an English announcement at each stop. Since the subway and buses do not run all night, you'll need to take a taxi for late-night travel. English -language subway maps are free and available upon request at major subway ticket counters.

bus
버스
beoseu

Seoul Metropolitan Government operates four easy to use color-coded bus types: blue, green, red, and yellow. Here is a detailed description of each bus.

Blue bus
간선버스
ganseonbeoseu

Inter-region rapid transit along major bus routes. Fixed rate for the first 10 km. Discount given when you pay with a T-money card.

Green bus
지선버스
jiseonbeoseu

Links inter-region rapid transit routes with subway lines within a region.

Red bus
광역버스
gwang-yeokbeoseu

Rapid transit between metropolitan areas, such as Seoul and Gyeonggi-do province or Incheon.

Yellow bus
순환버스
sunhwanbeoseu

Circular route within urban centers and metropolitan subcenters.

express bus
고속버스
gosokbeoseu

Express buses are an excellent way of traveling around the country. These buses are affordable, and you can purchase tickets without much hassle. Also, while car drivers suffer through traffic jams, buses can travel in dedicated high-occupancy lanes.

Four express bus terminals are located in Seoul, with service all over Korea. Each terminal has its own scheduled routes, so plan ahead and find the right terminal for your needs.

train

기차
gicha

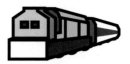

KORAIL standard train
(일반) 기차
(ilban) gicha

KORAIL standard trains are a low-cost means of traveling between cities. It takes five hours to travel from Seoul to the southernmost city of Busan. Standing tickets are also available if you you can't get a seat.

KTX (high-speed train)
케이티엑스 (고속철도)
keitiekseu (gosokcheoldo)

The Korea Train Express (KTX) costs more than a regular train but offers a fast and comfortable way to travel Korea. You can go from Seoul to Busan in under three hours, as opposed to the five hours it takes on the regular KORAIL train. Half the seats face backwards, so avoid these if you are prone to motion sickness. You can request forward-facing seats when you buy a ticket.

Ticket pre-sales are announced and carried out before major holidays. They often sell out well before the date of departure. Standing tickets are also available.

taxi

택시

taeksi

Taxis are relatively affordable, offering a speedy and comfortable means of transport around the city. There are two types of taxis: *ilban* and *mobeom*. Most offer free phone interpretation services, but it's a good idea to have your destination written down in Korean to show to the driver. Tipping is not required or expected.

taxi

(일반) 택시

(ilban) taeksi

Regular taxi. Starting fare is a fixed rate for the first 2 km. An additional charge of 20 percent is applied after midnight.

black luxury taxi / deluxe taxi

모범택시

mobeom taeksi

A more comfortable and friendlier ride than the regular taxi. As with regular taxis, tipping is not expected. Slightly more expensive than regular taxi service.

airport limousine bus

공항버스

gonghangbeoseu

The airport limousine bus service is a simple and economical way to travel from the airport to your destination, or vice versa. No reservation is required.

ASKING FOR DIRECTIONS

asking for directions
길 묻기
gil mutgi

Excuse me. I'd like to go to City Hall. How do I get there?

○ 실례합니다. 시청에 가고 싶은데 어떻게 가면 되죠?
sillyehamnida. sicheong-e gago sipeunde eotteoke gamyeon doejyo?

Excuse me. Is there a bus stop around here?

○ 저, 이 근처에 버스정류장이 있어요?
jeo, i geuncheo-e beoseujeongnyujang-i isseoyo?

I'm looking for the subway. Where can I find it?

○ 지하철역을 찾고 있는데, 어디로 가면 되죠?
jihacheoryeogeul chatgo inneunde, eodiro gamyeon doejyo?

Go straight along this road.

이 길을 따라 똑바로 가세요.

i gireul ttara ttokbaro gaseyo.

You should go back.

되돌아가세요.

doedoragaseyo.

Go left.

왼쪽으로 가세요.

oenjjogeuro gaseyo.

Go right.

오른쪽으로 가세요.

oreunjjogeuro gaseyo.

Turn right at the traffic light.

저 신호등 앞에서 오른쪽으로 가세요.

jeo sinhodeung apeseo oreunjjogeuro gaseyo.

Where am I?

여기가 어딘가요?

yeogiga oedin-gayo?

Can you write it down for me?

여기에 써 주실래요?

yeogie sseo jusillaeyo?

When asking for directions, provide the address in Korean, if possible. Carry a pen and paper and ask them to draw a map for you. A map app on your smartphone works well, too.

Where is Gansong Museum?

○ 간송미술관은 어디입니까?
gansong misulgwaneun eodiimnikka?

Right here.

○ 바로 여기입니다.
baro yeogiimnida.

Right over there.

○ 바로 저쪽에 있습니다.
baro jeojjoge itseumnida.

What floor is _____ located on?

○ _____은/는 몇 층에 있어요?
_____*eun/neun myeot cheung-e isseoyo?*

Which exit should I take for Kyobo Book Centre?

○ 교보문고로 가려면 어느 출구로 나가야 합니까?
gyobomun-goro garyeomyeon eoneu chulguro nagaya hamnikka?

How long does it take to walk there from here?

○ 여기서, 거기까지 걸어가는 데 얼마나 걸립니까?
yeogiseo geogikkaji georeoganeun de eolmana geollimnikka?

Most business cards and location maps do not reference street names unless they are major roads. Fortunately, major road signs are written in both Korean and English. Directions are given by describing adjacent buildings, landmarks, subway stations, and major intersections. Always bring the destination phone number in case you get lost.

Cardinal directions of north, south, east, and west are not used to provide directions as they are in Western countries.

BUSES & TAXIS

bus

버스
beoseu

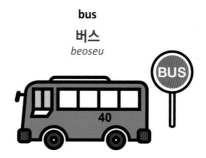

Does this bus go to Gangnam?

이 버스 강남에 갑니까?
i beosu gangname gamnikka?

No, this bus doesn't go there.

아니요. 안 갑니다.
aniyo. an gamnida.

So which bus should I take to go to Gangnam?

그럼, 몇 번 버스가 강남에 가요?
geureom, myeot beon beoseuga gangname gayo?

You should take bus number 407.

407번 버스를 타세요.
sabaekchilbeon beoseureul taseyo.

Does this bus go to Gwanghwamun?

이 버스 광화문에 갑니까?

i beosu gwanghwamune gamnikka?

Yes, this bus goes to Gwanghwamun. Please get on.

네, 갑니다. 타세요.

ne, gamnida. taseyo.

How many stops from here to Gwanghwamun?

여기서 광화문까지 몇 정거장이나 가야 하나요?

yeogiseo gwanghwamunkkaji myeot jeonggeojangina gaya hanayo?

Please tell me when we arrive.

도착하면 알려주세요.

dochakhamyeon allyeojuseyo.

You should get off at the next stop.

다음 정거장에서 내리세요.

da-eum jeonggeojangeseo naeriseyo.

taxi

택시

taeksi

TAXI

Would you take me to Sinchon?

○ 신촌까지 가주시겠어요?
  sinchonkkaji gajusigesseoyo?

Could you take me to Gimpo Airport?

○ 김포공항 부탁드려요.
  gimpogonghang butakdeuryeoyo.

How far is it to Hongik University?

○ 홍대까지 얼마나 멀죠?
  hongdaekkaji eolmana meoljyo?

I'm in a hurry.

○ 제가 급하거든요.
  jega geupageodeunyo.

Could you go a bit faster?

○ 좀 더 빨리 가주시겠어요?
  jom deo ppalli gajusigesseoyo?

Could you please go a bit slower?

○ 좀 천천히 가주세요.
  jom cheoncheonhi gajuseyo.

Turn right / left at the next intersection.

○ 이번 사거리에서 우회전 / 좌회전 해주세요.
  ibeon sageorieseo uhoejeon / jwahoejeon haejuseyo.

Please go about 100 meters down this side road.

○ 이 골목을 따라 100미터 정도 가주세요.
  i golmogeul ttara baengmiteo jeongdo gajuseyo. .

Please let me out in front of the crosswalk.

저 횡단보도 앞에서 세워주세요.
jeo hoengdanbodo apeseo sewojuseyo.

You can stop here, please.

여기서 세워주세요.
yeogiseo sewojuseyo.

Sir / Madam, we've arrived. You should get out here.

손님, 다 왔습니다. 여기서 내리세요.
sonnim, da watseumnida. yeogiseo naeriseyo.

How much is it?

얼마죠?
eolmajyo?

In order to provide better service for visitors, the Seoul Metropolitan Government launched an official foreign language taxi service. This reservation-based service offers drivers who speak English, Japanese, and / or Chinese. Fares are 20 percent higher than with standard taxis but can be paid with cash, T-money cards, or major international credit cards. These taxis can also be chartered at flat rates for periods of several hours or more. You can find them conveniently stationed at Incheon International Airport, but phone or internet reservations are recommended. (http://www.internationaltaxi.co.kr, Phone: 82-1644-2255)

Most taxis are equipped with GPS navigation systems, but it's unusual to see drivers utilizing of them. Be aware of landmarks or nearby intersections and bring along destination contact information just in case.

SUBWAYS & TRAINS

subway

지하철
jihacheol

Could I have an English subway map, please?

◌ 영어 지하철 노선도 좀 주세요.
Yeong-eo jihacheol noseondo jom juseyo.

Which line should I take to go to Jongno?

◌ 종로에 가려고 하는데, 몇 호선을 타야 하나요?
jongno-e garyeogo haneunde, myeot toseoneul taya hanayo?

Tickets can be purchased at machines near the subway entrance. As of 2013 , a deposit fee of 500 won is charged for the card. After selecting your destination, the machine will request a cash payment. The cost of the trip will depend on the distance, but the base fare for adults is 1,050 won for the first 10 km. You can get a refund for the 500 won deposit after your trip at one of the deposit refund machines.
Seoul Metro English website: http://www.seoulmetro.co.kr/eng/

exit / way out
나가는 곳 / 출구
naganeun got / chulgu

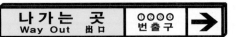

You should take Line 1 (the dark blue line).

○ 지하철 1호선을 타세요.
jihacheol ilhoseoneul taseyo.

Which exit should I take if I want to go to Sejong Center?

○ 세종문화회관으로 가려면 몇 번 출구로 나가면 될까요?
sejongmunhwahoegwaneuro garyeomyeon myeot beon chulguro nagamyeon doelkkayo?

When does the last train on Line 2 leave for Hongik University?

○ 홍대입구역으로 가는 2호선 마지막 열차가 몇 시에 있나요?
hongdaeipguyeogeuro ganeun ihoseon majimak yeolchaga myeot sie innayo?

Which line should I transfer to if I want to go to Myeongdong?

○ 명동에 가려는데 몇 호선으로 갈아타야 하나요?
myeongdong-e garyeoneunde myeot toseoneuro garataya hanayo?

You should take Line 4 to Danggogae.

○ 4호선 당고개 방면으로 가세요.
sahoseon danggogae bangmyeoneuro gaseyo.

---

transfer

환승
hwanseung

←7호선 갈아타는곳 Transfer to Line7
7 號線 換乘

Where do I go to transfer to Line 4?

○ 4호선으로 갈아타려면 어디로 가야 하나요?
sahoseoneuro garataryeomyeon eodiro gaya hanayo?

Follow the blue line on the wall to transfer to Line 4.

○ 4호선으로 갈아타려면 벽의 파란색 라인을 따라가세요.
sahoseoneuro garataryeomyeon byeogui paransaek raineul ttaragaseyo.

Please have a seat.

○ 여기 앉으세요.
yeogi anjeuseyo.

Show good manners by giving up your seat to handicapped people, senior citizens, pregnant women, and mothers with young children.

train

기차
gicha

Where can I buy a train ticket?

기차표는 어디에서 살 수 있죠?
gichapyoneun eodieseo sal su itjyo?

The ticket counter is over there.

매표소는 저쪽입니다.
maepyosoneun jeojjogimnida.

One ticket for Busan, please.

부산행 표 한 장 주세요.
busanhaeng pyo han jang juseyo.

Is that one-way or round trip?

편도입니까, 왕복입니까?
pyeondoimnikka, wangbogimnikka?

What time would you like to depart?

몇 시 표로 드릴까요?
myeot si pyoro deurilkkayo?

The earliest train available, please.

제일 빨리 출발하는 열차표로 주세요.

jeil ppalli chulbalhaneun yeolchapyoro juseyo.

Sorry, that train is sold out.

죄송합니다. 기차표가 매진되었습니다.

joesonghamnida, gichapyoga maejindoe-eotseumnida.

How long does it take to get to Daejeon on KTX?

KTX로는 대전까지 시간이 얼마나 걸리죠?

keitiekseuroneun daejeonkkaji sigani eolmana geollijyo?

Is there a cheaper ticket than on the KTX?

KTX말고 좀 더 싼 표도 있나요?

keitiekseu malgo jom deo ssan pyodo innayo?

Excuse me. Can you tell me which platform to go to for the 6:15 train to Busan?

실례지만, 부산행 6시 15분 기차는 어느 플랫폼에서 타나요?

sillyejiman, busanhaeng yeoseot si sibo bun gichaneun eoneu peullaetpomeseo tanayo?

Please show me your train ticket.

기차표를 보여주세요.

gichapyoreul boyeojuseyo.

Is there a dining car on this train?

이 기차에 식당 칸이 있습니까?

i gicha-e sikdang kani itseumnikka?

AIRPORTS & AIR TRAVEL

leaving the country

출국
chulguk

Where is the check-in counter?

○ 탑승수속 카운터가 어디죠?
tapseungsusok kaunteoga eodijyo?

A window seat, please.

○ 창가 좌석 부탁드립니다.
changkka jwaseok butakdeurimnida.

How many bags are you checking in?

○ 짐을 몇 개나 부치실 겁니까?
jimeul myeot gaena buchisil geomnikka?

Are there any liquids in your bag?

○ 가방에 액체가 있나요?
gabang-e aekchega innayo?

Please take your laptop out of your bag.

○ 가방에서 컴퓨터를 꺼내주세요.
gabang-eseo keompyuteoreul kkeonaejuseyo.

Show me your passport and ticket.

○ 여권과 탑승권을 보여주세요.
yeokkwongwa tapseungkkwoneul boyeojuseyo.

on the airplane

비행기 안에서
bihaenggi aneseo

Please turn off all portable electronic devices before takeoff.

○ 이륙하는 동안 휴대용 전자장비를 꺼주세요.
iryukhaneun dong-an hyudaeyong jeonjajangbireul kkeojuseyo.

What would you like to eat?

○ 식사는 어떤 것으로 하시겠습니까?
siksaneun eotteon geoseuro hasigetseumnikka?

Could you please bring me water?

○ 물 좀 갖다 주세요.
mul jom gatda juseyo.

Do you have an English-language newspaper?

○ 영자 신문 있나요?
yeongjja sinmun innayo?

entering Korea

입국
ipguk

How long are you staying in Korea?

○ 한국에 얼마나 머물 건가요?
han-guge eolmana meomul geon-gayo?

Could I have an arrival card?

○ 입국 카드를 좀 주시겠어요?
ipkkuk kadeureul jom jusigesseoyo?

Are you here for business or vacation?

○ 한국에는 업무로 오셨습니까, 아니면 휴가로 오셨습니까?
han-gugeneun eommuro osyeotseumnikka, animyeon hyugaro osyeotseumnikka?

Can you tell me where I can claim my baggage?

○ 수하물 찾는 곳이 어디입니까?
suhamul channeun gosi eodiimnikka?

I've been waiting at the baggage claim area for about thirty minutes now, but I can't locate my bags.

○ 제가 약 30분 정도 짐 찾는 곳에서 기다렸는데 제 가방들이 안 보이네요.
jega yak samsipbun jeongdo jim channeun goseseo gidaryeonneunde je gabangdeuri an boineyo.

Do you have anything to declare?

○ 세관에 신고할 물품이 있습니까?
segwane singohal mulpumi itseumnikka?

No, I don't.

○ 아니오, 없습니다.
anio, eopseumnida.

Where can I take the airport limousine bus to downtown Seoul?

○ 서울 시내로 가는 공항버스는 어디에서 타죠?
seoul sinaero ganeun gonghangbeoseuneun eodieseo tajyo?

There's an airport limousine bus stop right in front of Gate 2.

○ 게이트 2번으로 나가시면 바로 앞에 공항버스 정류장이 있습니다.
geiteu ibeoneuro nagasimyeon baro ape gonghangbeoseu jeongnyujangi itseumnida.

ASKING FOR DIRECTIONS

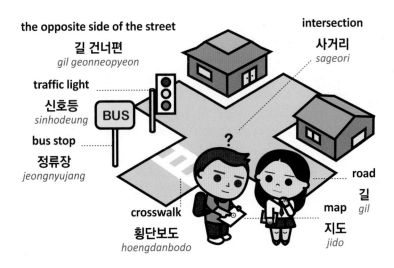

the opposite side of the street
길 건너편
gil geonneopyeon

traffic light
신호등
sinhodeung

bus stop
정류장
jeongnyujang

intersection
사거리
sageori

road
길
gil

map
지도
jido

crosswalk
횡단보도
hoengdanbodo

over there
저쪽에
jeojjoge

here
여기에
yeogie

SUBWAYS

subway station
지하철역
jihacheoryeok

English subway map
영어 지하철 노선도
yeongeo jihacheol noseondo

a single journey ticket
1회용 교통카드
ilhoeyong gyotongkadeu

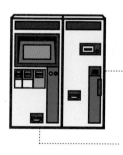

ticket vending machine
교통카드 충전기
gyotongkadeu chungjeon-gi

card deposit refund machine
보증금 환급기
bojeunggeum hwangeupgi

TRAINS

ticket counter
매표소
maepyoso

round trip
왕복
wangbok

one-way trip
편도
pyeondo

train ticket
기차표
gichapyo

AIRPORTS & AIR TRAVEL

takeoff
이륙
iryuk

seat belt
안전벨트
anjeonbelteu

landing
착륙
changnyuk

passport
여권
yeogwon

international flight
국제선
gukjeseon

domestic flight
국내선
gungnaeseon

airplane ticket
비행기표
bihaenggipyo

seat(s)
좌석
jwaseok

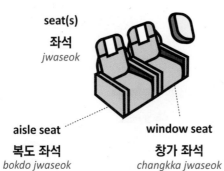

aisle seat
복도 좌석
bokdo jwaseok

window seat
창가 좌석
changkka jwaseok

emergency exit
비상 탈출구
bisang talchulgu

beverage
음료
eumnyo

snacks
스낵 / 간식
seunaek / gansik

captain / pilot
조종사
jojongsa

flight attendant
승무원
seungmuwon

meal

식사

siksa

immigration

출입국 관리소

churipguk gwalliso

baggage claim

수하물 찾는 곳

suhamul channeun got

carry-on luggage

기내 휴대 수하물

ginae hyudae suhamul

customs

세관

segwan

customs declaration form

세관 신고 카드

segwan sin-go kadeu

bag

가방

gabang

T-MONEY CARD & PROXY DRIVER

T-money card

티 머니 카드

ti meoni kadeu

T-money is a rechargeable electronic payment system for use on Seoul public transportation: buses, subways, taxis, and even parking garages.

When you use the T-money card you'll automatically receive discounts on bus and subway rides within the Seoul metro area. Seoul and its surroundings have an integrated fare system with no charge for transfers between different types of public transportation. Passengers pay a flat fee for distances over 10km, no matter how often they change buses (including village buses) and subway trains within 30 minutes of their transfer time. An additional charge of 100 won is added every 5 km. To receive a discount, you will need to tap your T-money card against the reader when you get on and off the bus (or subway line). Scan your card at every transfer entrance and exit, and any necessary fare adjustments will be made automatically.

Many Korean credit cards have a built-in T-money feature. This is ultra-convenient, as the card doesn't require you to keep a balance, and your trips are automatically listed out for you on your monthly statement.

proxy driver

대리운전
daeri unjeon

This is a call service for when you've driven your car after drinking alcohol. It's a cost-effective way to get both you and your car home safely. Sometimes it's cheaper than taxi.

FOOD &
RESTAURANTS

4 FOOD & RESTAURANTS

OVERVIEW Places to Eat and Eating Etiquette

Places to Eat in Korea

Korean food is famous for its flavors and healthy ingredients. You'll find a variety of dishes to suit your tastes, as well as a broad range of restaurants to meet any budget.

Korean barbecue
고기집
gogijip

Serves pork or beef cooked on charcoal, a stone slate, or a mesh grill. The meat comes plain or marinated. A charcoal grill is preferred over the mesh-style gas grill but costs more.

street snack stall
포장마차
pojangmacha

Outdoor tents and small shacks that offer cheap snacks and meals. Some are standing room only, while others have limited seating on patio-style furniture.

Korean restaurant
한식집
hansikjip

A variety of traditional Korean meals can be found here.

family restaurant
레스토랑
reseutorang

A general word for any place to eat but typically associated with foreign food.

snack bar
분식집
bunsikjip

Serves small meals and snacks on the cheap, including spicy rice cakes (*tteokbokki*), batter-dipped foods, and instant noodle (*ramyeon*).

tavern / bar
호프/바
hopeu/ba

These establishments serve a variety of drinks, including Korean beer and soju. Normally, you're expected to order at least one small dish of food (*anju*).

Café
카페
kape

Offers various coffees, teas, and desserts. A popular dish to accompany your beverage is a waffle covered in fruit and ice cream. Perfect for sharing.

Eating Etiquette

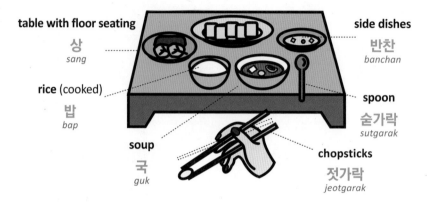

table with floor seating
상
sang

rice (cooked)
밥
bap

soup
국
guk

side dishes
반찬
banchan

spoon
숟가락
sutgarak

chopsticks
젓가락
jeotgarak

In Korea, it's important to use traditional phrases when you eat with others. Before the meal, say 잘 먹겠습니다 (*jal meokgesseumnida*), which literally means "I gratefully receive." After the meal, say 잘 먹었습니다 (*jal meogeosseumnida*), which means "thank you for the meal."

At the beginning of the meal, bowls of rice and soup are normally served to each person. Dishes are not passed around, and it's good manners to serve those around you first. It's also good manners to put the food from the serving dish onto your plate. You shouldn't eat directly from the serving dish. It's uncommon to hold a bowl of soup up to your mouth as you might in China and Japan. Bring the food to your mouth rather than the other way around.

Knives aren't placed on the table, and they're generally not needed, as meals are cut into bite-sized portions. Use your chopsticks to cut or tear when necessary. Korean chopsticks are flat metal blades that can easily pull meat apart. As in Western countries, avoid talking with your mouth full.

Toothpicks are typically found near the cash register. If you need to use one, make sure to turn your head away from other people or cover your mouth with your free hand. Similarly, you may notice women covering their mouths with one hand while chewing. This is considered good etiquette as well.

Traditionally, excessive chatting during mealtime was frowned upon in Korean culture. Times have changed, but don't be surprised to see the older guests focused on their meals and not on you.

Always wait for the oldest members to be seated and begin eating first. If they are the last to finish, everyone should remain seated until they are done. Pace yourself. Through some work of magic, Koreans all finish their meals in about the same amount of time.

Enjoy your meal!

맛있게 드세요!

masitge deuseyo!

Don't!

blow your nose

코 풀기

ko pulgi

talk with your mouth full

음식 입에 가득 넣고 말하기

eumsik ibe gadeuk neoko malhagi

ARRIVING AT THE RESTAURANT & ORDERING FOOD

restaurant

음식점
eumsikjeom

Welcome! How many people are in your party?

○ 어서 오세요. 몇 분이세요?
eoseo oseyo. myeot buniseyo?

There are four of us.

○ 4명이요.
nemyeong-iyo.

Could we have a seat in the non-smoking / smoking section, please?

◯ 금연석 / 흡연석으로 부탁드려요.

geumyeonseok / heubyeonseok-euro butakdeuryeoyo.

Would you please have a seat over here?

◯ 이쪽으로 앉으시겠어요?

ijjogeuro anjeusigesseoyo?

Can I see the menu, please?

◯ 메뉴판 좀 주세요.

menyupan jom juseyo.

Do you have an English-language menu?

◯ 영어 메뉴판도 있나요?

yeong-eo menyupando innayo?

Here is the menu.

◯ 여기 메뉴판 있습니다.

yeogi menyupan itseumnida.

What kind of food would you like to have?

◯ 어떤 음식 드시겠어요?

eotteon eumsik deusigesseoyo?

What will you have?

◯ 뭐 드시고 싶으세요?

mwo deusigo sipeuseyo?

Are you okay with spicy food?

◯ 매운 음식도 괜찮으시겠어요?

Mae-un eumsikdo gwaenchaneusigesseoyo?

ordering food
음식 주문
eumsik jumun

Would you like to order?

◌ 주문하시겠습니까?
jumunhasigetseumnikka?

We're ready to order.

◌ 이제 주문할게요.
ije jumunhalkkeyo.

Excuse me, I am / we are ready to order.

◌ 여기, 주문 좀 받아주세요.
yeogi, jumun jom badajuseyo.

What's your specialty?

◌ 여기 뭐가 맛있어요?
yeogi mwoga masisseoyo?

Which foods aren't spicy?

◌ 안 매운 음식은 뭐가 있죠?
an mae-un eumsigeun mwoga itjyo?

We'd / I'd like four servings of short ribs of pork.

돼지갈비 4인분 주세요.
dwaejigalbi sainbun juseyo.

One serving of kimchi stew, please.

김치찌개 1인분 부탁드려요.
gimchijjigae irinbun butakdeuryeoyo.

I'd like this.

이걸로 주세요.
igeollo juseyo.

Could you please bring more of this dish?

이 반찬 좀 더 부탁드려요.
i banchan jom deo butakdeuryeoyo.

Could we please have two more servings of Bulgogi?

불고기 2인분 추가요.
bulgogi iirinbun chugayo.

Could I please have a fork?

포크 좀 부탁드려요.
pokeu jom butakdeuryeoyo.

Could I please have some more water?

물 좀 더 주시겠어요?
mul jom deo jusigesseoyo?

Where is the restroom?

화장실이 어디죠?
hwajangsiri eodijyo?

takeout

음식 포장
eumsik pojang

Do you do takeout?

○ 음식 포장 되나요?
eumsik pojang doenayo?

Can I have a takeout container.

○ 남은 음식 좀 싸 갈게요.
nameun eumsik jom ssa galgeyo.

Korean food is normally shared with everyone at the table. You should serve the oldest members of your party first and wait for them to begin eating before you do.

While eating, you're unlikely to experience any interruptions by restaurant staff. That's because Koreans prefer to eat without being disturbed. When you need service, simply raise your hand or politely call out for assistance. Someone is always within eyesight. Calling out to your server is culturally acceptable.

MAKING COMPLAINTS & PAYING THE BILL

making complaints
항의
hangui

We've been waiting a really long time.
너무 오래 기다렸어요.
neomu orae gidaryeosseoyo.

We've been waiting 30 minutes and the food still hasn't arrived.
주문한 지 30분이 지났는데도 아직 음식이 안 나왔어요.
jumunhan ji samsipbuni jinanneundedo ajik eumsigi an nawasseoyo.

I didn't order this.
이건 제가 시킨 게 아닌 것 같은데요.
igeon jega sikin ge anin geot gateundeyo.

I ordered the steak medium rare. This is overcooked.
저는 미디엄 레어를 시켰는데 이 고기는 너무 익었네요.
jeo-neun midieom re-eoreul sikyeonneunde i gogineun neomu igeonneyo.

This stew is cold.

이 찌개 식었네요.
i jjigae sigeonneyo.

I think this side dish is spoiled.

이 반찬 상한 것 같은데요.
i banchan sanghan geot gateundeyo.

There's something in this cup. Could I have a clean one, please?

이 컵에 이상한 게 있어요. 컵 좀 바꿔주세요.
i keobe isanghan ge isseoyo. keop jom bakkwojuseyo

There's a hair in this side dish.

반찬에서 머리카락이 나왔어요.
banchaneseo meorikaragi nawasseoyo.

It's on me. / I'm buying. / It's my treat.

오늘은 제가 살게요.
oneureun jega salkkeyo.

Where can I pay?

계산은 어디서 하나요?
gyesaneun eodiseo hanayo?

Can I have the check, please?

계산서 좀 부탁합니다.
gyesanseo jom butakhamnida.

Do you accept credit cards?

신용카드 받습니까?
sinyongkadeu batseumnikka?

paying for the meal

음식값 계산
eumsikgap gyesan

May I have a receipt, please?

영수증 좀 부탁드려요.
yeongsujeung jom butakdeuryeoyo.

Thank you for the meal.

잘 먹었습니다.
jal meogeotseumnida.

Korean food is delicious.

한국 음식 참 맛있네요.
han-guk eumsik, cham masinneyo.

Family restaurants, hotels, and fine dining establishments will collect your payment at the table. These places also add a 10 percent VAT at the time of payment (check the fine print at the bottom of the menu).

Typical Korean restaurants, however, require you to bring the check directly to the register near the entrance. Tipping is not customary in Korea.

COFFEE SHOPS & TEAHOUSES

coffee shops

커피숍
keopisyop

Welcome! What would you like?
○ 어서 오세요. 무엇으로 드릴까요?
eoseo oseyo. mueoseuro deurilkkayo?

I'd like an Americano, please.
○ 아메리카노 한 잔만 주세요.
amerikano han janman juseyo.

One caffè latte, please.
○ 카페라떼 하나 주세요.
kaperatte hana juseyo.

One cappuccino to go, please.
○ 카푸치노 하나, 테이크아웃이요.
kapuchino hana, teikeuausiyo.

Korean teahouses

전통찻집
jeontongchatjip

A double shot of espresso, please.
○ 에스프레소 투 샷 진하게요.
eseupeureso tu syat jinhageyo.

Do you want it hot or cold?
○ 따뜻한 것으로 드릴까요? 시원한 것으로 드릴까요?
ttatteutan geoseuro deurilkkayo? siwonhan geoseuro deurilkkayo?

I'd like a glass of iced green tea, please.
○ 아이스 녹차 한 잔 주세요.
aiseu nokcha han jan juseyo.

I'd like a cup of ginseng tea, please.
○ 인삼차 한 잔 주세요.
insamcha han jan juseyo.

Could you please add some simple syrup?

○ 시럽 좀 넣어 주시겠어요?
sireop jom neo-eo jusigesseoyo?

Could I have some whipped cream on that?

○ 위에 생크림 좀 얹어주시겠어요?
wie saengkeurim jom eonjeojusigesseoyo?

This coffee doesn't taste good.

○ 커피 맛이 좀 이상해요.
keopi masi jom isanghaeyo.

I'd like a loyalty card.

○ 포인트 카드 주세요.
pointeu kadeu juseyo.

Can I redeem this loyalty card for a cup of coffee?

○ 이 포인트 카드 커피로 교환해 주세요.
i pointeu kadeu keopiro gyohwanhae juseyo.

Most coffee shops have their own loyalty cards, where purchasing 10 to 12 cups of coffee (or so) will get you one for free. Coffee shops are open later than most restaurants, which makes them great places to meet friends or relax and surf the internet. Some are even open for 24 hours!

Many neighborhoods also have small, inexpensive takeout-only coffee shops. The quality is often good, as the coffee beans are freshly ground for each order.

MAKING RESERVATIONS & ORDERING TAKEOUT

reservations

예약
yeyak

I would like to make a reservation.

○ 예약을 하고 싶어요.
yeyageul hago sipeoyo.

For which day and for what time?

○ 예약을 원하시는 날짜와 시간을 말씀해 주세요.
yeyageul wonhasineun naljjawa siganeul malsseumhae juseyo.

Tonight at 7:30 pm, please.

오늘 밤, 7시 반이요.
oneul bam, ilgobsi baniyo.

How many people is this reservation for?

몇 분 예약하시겠습니까?
myeot bun yeyakhasigetseumnikka?

I would like to make a reservation for six people.

여섯 사람 예약하고 싶은데요.
yeoseot saram yeyakhago sipeundeyo.

Can I request a table by the window?

창 쪽으로 자리를 예약할 수 있나요?
chang jjogeuro jarireul yeyakhal su innayo?

I'd like to make a lunchtime reservation for two for tomorrow.

내일 점심 때, 2명 예약하고 싶은데요.
naeil jeomsim ttae, dumyeong yeyakhago sipeundeyo.

I'm sorry, we're all booked at that time.

죄송합니다. 그 시간 예약은 다 찼습니다.
joesonghamnida. geu sigan yeyageun da chatseumnida.

Do you have parking?

주차가 가능한가요?
juchaga ganeunghan-gayo?

Yes, we do.

네, 가능합니다.
ne, ganeunghamnida.

Seoul has one of the world's highest concentrations of restaurants per capita. Company dinners are a frequent affair, and tables with floor seating can easily accommodate large groups of office workers.

On most days, reservations are not required, even for parties of four or more. But for weekend evenings, holidays, or at trendy places, it's best to call ahead. If you're visiting a barbecue restaurant for lunch, reservations will ensure that the side dishes and tableware are ready and that you'll have plenty of time to eat before returning to work. For your convenience, many Seoul restaurants offer valet parking, with an obligatory tip of 1,000 to 2,000 won.

ordering takout
배달 음식 주문하기
baedal eumsik jumunhagi

Hello?
여보세요?
yeoboseyo?

Is this the Pizza House?

○ 피자집이죠?
pijajibijyo?

I'd like one large combination pizza delivered.

○ 콤비네이션 피자 큰 거로 하나 배달해 주세요.
kombineisyeon pija keun georo hana baedalhae juseyo.

Can I have a cola, too?

○ 콜라도 하나 갖다 주시겠어요?
kollado hana gatda jusigesseoyo?

Is this a Chinese restaurant?

○ 중국집이죠?
junggukjibijyo?

Could we have one large order of sweet-and-sour pork and one serving of fried rice?

○ 탕수육 큰 거 하나랑 볶음밥 하나 부탁드려요.
tangsuyuk keun geo hanarang bokkeumbap hana butakdeuryeoyo.

What's the total?

○ 합해서 얼마죠?
hapaeseo eolmajyo?

Can I pay with a credit card?

○ 신용카드 사용이 가능한가요?
sinyongkadeu sayong-i ganeunghan-gayo?

What is your address?

○ 주소가 어떻게 되시죠?
jusoga eotteoke doesijyo?

138-7 Hwa-dong, Jongno Gu. It's on the second floor.

○ 종로구 화동 138–7번지, 2층입니다.
jongnogu hwadong baeksamsippaldasichilbeonji, icheung-imnida.

Please speak more slowly.

○ 좀 천천히 얘기해 주세요.
jom cheoncheonhi yaegihae juseyo.

The food delivery system in Korea is unique in that many types of food are available for quick delivery. Popular ones are pizza, chicken, BBQ, and Chinese food.

If you plan to pay the deliveryman with a credit card, make sure to mention that when you place your order, as he'll have to bring a card reader with him. Usually a minimum purchase of 10,000 won may be required if you're using your card to pay. Tipping is not customary, and while most places accept credit cards, it's best to confirm by phone first.

POPULAR KOREAN MEAT DISHES

Korean barbecued short ribs of pork / beef
돼지갈비 / 소갈비
dwaejigalbi / sogalbi

Choose pork or beef to be cooked on a gas or charcoal table grill. Marinated and non-marinated meats are available. The marinades are slightly sweet and consist of onions, garlic, water, sugar, and soy sauce. Asian minced pear and other fruits may be used in the marinade as well. Dip the grilled meat into the soy dipping sauce or a mixture of salt and pepper, if you're served one. Now place the meat on a green lettuce or a sesame leaf. Pickled onions, spicy sauce, and other ingredients can be added on top. Fold the lettuce wrap with your fingers and enjoy.

POPULAR KOREAN RICE DISHES

rice with mixed vegetables
비빔밥
bibimbap

Bibimbap can be described as a bowl of rice mixed with various vegetables, and sometimes meat. Chili pepper paste and an egg are signature items that you mix in at the table. Bibimbap can be served in a plastic or metal bowl.

kimchi fried rice
김치볶음밥
gimchibokkeumbap

Chopped kimchi and various meats are pan-fried with rice. Other ingredients include green onions, garlic, regular onions, and sesame oil. A fried egg is placed sunny-side-up on top of the dish.

POPULAR KOREAN STEWS

kimchi stew
김치찌개
gimchijjigae

Kimchi *jjigae*, or kimchi stew, is made with kimchi and other ingredients such as scallions, onions, diced tofu, pork, or seafood. It's often prepared with older, more fermented and "riper" kimchi, creating a much stronger taste and adding a high content of the "good" bacteria that's found in yogurt.

soybean paste stew
된장찌개
doenjangjjigae

Doenjang jjigae is the Korean equivalent of Japanese miso soup. Both are made using fermented soybean paste. *Doenjang jjigae* has green onions in a vegetable or beef broth, compared to miso's fish-based broth. It's an excellent source of protein.

army stew
부대찌개
budaejjigae

Budae jjigae, or "army stew," is a Korean dish that uses typical US Army rations such as hot dogs, beans, ground beef, and Spam. The ingredients are mixed together in a spicy broth; *ramyeon* is often thrown in as well.

marinated beef in a clay bowl
뚝배기 불고기
ttukbaegi bulgogi

Beef stew with vegetables and noodles. Cooked and served in an earthenware bowl with green onions, mushrooms, and cellophane noodles. Not spicy.

POPULAR KOREAN NOODLES

japchae
잡채
japchae

Cellophane noodles, or *dangmyeon*, as they are known in Korea, are made from sweet potato starch. The noodles are pan fried in a mixture of soy sauce, sugar, sesame oil, and finely cut vegetables. Not spicy.

cold noodle soup
물냉면
mullaengmyeon

A popular summertime food. Buckwheat noodles are served in an ice-cold soup with egg, mustard, and vinegar.

spicy noodles
비빔국수
bibimguksu

Cold *somyeon* noodles are served on a dish with chili pepper paste, minced garlic, sugar, and vinegar. Spicy.

black-bean-sauce noodles
자장면
jajangmyeon

This Korean-style Chinese dish is made with wheat noodles in a black bean sauce.

POPULAR KOREAN SIDE DISHES

Nearly every Korean meal includes an assortment of side dishes collectively known as *banchan*. More expensive meals will almost always include a larger variety of side dishes. And while you can't ask your waitress to bring more of the main dish, you can ask for more side dishes at no additional cost.

cabbage kimchi
배추김치
baechugimchi

Pickled cabbage is a staple food for Koreans and is associated internationally with its Korean origins. Kimchi is a fermented mixture of ingredients that includes red pepper powder, cabbage, green onions, radishes, and garlic. The garlic aids in preventing cancer, reduces the risk of heart disease, and minimizes the effects of aging. It's also recognized for lowering cholesterol levels in the body.

radish kimchi
깍두기
kkakdugi

Peeled and cubed daikon radish served in a sauce made from red pepper powder, scallions, ginger, minced garlic, salt, and sugar. As with all types of kimchi, it's best served slightly chilled.

seasoned bean sprouts
콩나물무침
kongnamulmuchim

Boiled bean sprouts seasoned with salt, garlic, green onions, and sesame oil. Served cool.

pan-fried fish cake
어묵볶음
eomukbokkeum

Ground fish that's been pan fried and sprinkled with sesame seeds.

COFFEE

coffee beans
커피콩, 원두
keopikong, wondu

espresso machine
에스프레소 머신
eseupeureso meosin

milk foam
우유 거품
uyu geopum

coffee
커피
keopi

americano
아메리카노
amerikano

latte
라떼
ratte

cappuccino
카푸치노
kapuchino

café mocha
모카 커피
moka keopi

espresso
에스프레소
eseupeureso

instant coffee
커피 믹스
keopi mikseu

coffee filter
커피 필터
keopi pilteo

simple syrup
시럽
sireop

KOREAN TEA

Korean tea
한국 전통차
hanguk jeontongcha

green tea
녹차
nokcha

ginseng tea
인삼차
insamcha

The Korean name literally translates as "green tea." Filled with antioxidants that help minimize the effects of aging.

Normally purchased in powder form from supermarkets and department stores. Ginseng contains adaptogens that can help you manage stress, fatigue, and anxiety.

ginger tea
생강차
saenggangcha

Recommended for preventing colds; treating headaches, motion sickness, or diarrhea; and maintaining a healthy physique.

citron tea
유자차
yujacha

Made from an East Asian citrus fruit called *yuja* that resembles a grapefruit. It's sliced and mixed with honey or sugar before preserving.

plum tea
매실차
maesilcha

This sweet drink is sometimes served as a dessert after large meals.

barley tea
보리차
boricha

Commonly served as a complimentary tea in Korean restaurants. Naturally caffeine-free and good for treating stomach aches.

ssanghwa herbal tea
쌍화차
ssanghwacha

A healthy tea made from various Korean herbs. Useful in fighting colds and exhaustion.

corn tea
옥수수차
oksusucha

Kernels of corn are roasted and then boiled to make this drink. It has a naturally sweet taste and is often combined with barley tea.

STREET FOOD

street vendor

포장마차
pojangmacha

Typically located near busy intersections and nightlife areas, these food carts and stalls offer quick, inexpensive food all year round. There are daytime and nighttime types, and hours vary by location and owner. Some of the nighttime *pojangamacha* shops even serve alcohol. Types of food also vary.

In the fall and winter months, these carts and stalls are sealed up like a tent, offering a warm haven from the cold. Weather conditions aside, Koreans love this kind of comfort food.

Excuse me.

저기요.
jeogiyo.

How much is one serving of *tteokbokki*?

떡볶이 1인분에 얼마예요?
tteokbokki irinbune eolmayeyo?

tteokbokki
(spicy rice cake stir-fry)
떡볶이
tteokbokki

Arguably the most popular Korean street food, *tteokbokki* is large, chewy, rectangular rice cake mixed in a hot pepper sauce with scallions.

skewered fish cake
어묵 / 오뎅
eomuk / odeng

Fish cake pieces boiled in broth and speared with a skewer. The cake, which is made by mixing flour and ground fish, is also used in dishes such as *tteokbokki*.

Korean blood sausage
순대
sundae

Similar to European blood sausage, it's made from pig intestines and stuffed with cellophane noodles, congealed pork blood, and spices.

batter-dipped foods
튀김
twigim

Deep-fried vegetables and seafood covered in a thick and hearty batter. Squid, sweet potatoes, chili peppers, and dumplings are the most common types served.

seaweed rolls
김밥
gimbap

Rolled seaweed stuffed with boiled white rice and various other ingredients. These often include imitation crab meat, cucumber, pickled radish, and carrot.

Korean pancakes
부침개
buchimgae

Enjoyed as a snack, appetizer, or side dish, pancakes are made from a variety of ingredients including kimchi, green onions, seafood, and meat.

PREPARING FOR LIFE IN KOREA

OVERVIEW Your Alien Registration Card

Your alien registration card functions much like a social security card in the US. It's required to set up apartment utilities or make a mobile phone contract.

To obtain an alien card, you need the following items: an application, your passport, two passport photos (3.5 x 4.5 cm), documents supporting your stay in Korea, and a processing fee of 10,000 won. Before processing, you should make a photocopy of your passport for emergency use.

Your alien registration card ID number consists of 13 digits. The first six digits represent your birth date in year-month-day format (for example, April 1, 1990, is 900401). The first digit after the dash represents your nationality and gender. A leading 1 means a Korean male, 2 means a Korean female, 5 means a foreign male, and 6 means a foreign female.

Korean Immigration Service: http://www.immigration.go.kr/

RENTING A HOUSE

real estate agency

부동산 중개소

budongsan junggaeso

I'm looking for a two-bedroom apartment.

○ 방 두 개짜리 아파트를 보러 왔어요.

bang du gaejjari apateureul boreo wasseoyo.

What are house prices like around Hannam-dong?

○ 한남동은 가격이 어느 정도 합니까?

hannamdong-eun gagyeogi eoneu jeongdo hamnikka?

Will you be buying or renting?

○ 집을 사실 건가요? 아니면 빌리실 건가요?

jibeul sasil geon-gayo? animyeon billisil geon-gayo?

Do you want a lump sum rental or a monthly fee rental?

○ 월세를 원하세요? 전세를 원하세요?

wolsereul wonhaseyo? jeonsereul wonhaseyo?

security deposit
보증금
bojeunggeum

monthly fee
월세
wolse

I'm looking for a monthly fee rental.

월세요.
wolseyo.

What's your budget?

비용은 얼마를 예상하세요?
biyong-eun eolmareul yesanghaseyo?

I can pay a deposit of 20,000,000 won and monthly rent of around 400,000.

보증금은 2,000만 원, 월세는 40만 원 정도였으면 좋겠어요.
bojeunggeumeun icheonman won, wolseneun sasimman won jeongdoyeosseumyeon jokesseoyo.

An apartment matching your criteria just came onto the market.

마침 같은 조건의 아파트가 나와 있어요.
machim gateun jokkeonui apateuga nawa isseoyo.

How close is the nearest subway station?

지하철역에서 얼마나 가깝나요?

jihacheoryeogeseo eolmana gakkamnayo?

It's a 20-minute walk or five minutes by village bus.

지하철역에서 걸어서 20분 정도 걸립니다. 마을버스를 타면 5분 걸려요.

jihacheoryeogeseo georeoseo isipbun jeongdo geollimnida. ma-eulbeoseureul tamyeon o bun geollyeoyo.

I'm looking for a place with access to the subway.

지하철역에서 좀 더 가까웠으면 좋겠어요.

jihacheoryeogeseo jom deo gakkawosseumyeon jokesseoyo.

Apartments near subway stations are always more expensive.

지하철역에서 가까운 곳은 더 비쌉니다.

jihacheoryeogeseo gakkaun goseun deo bissamnida.

There are two types of apartment leases in Korea. One is a monthly rental arrangement that's similar to the Western rental system. A refundable security deposit, which is often 10 to 20 times the monthly rent fee, is required up front. Ten percent of the deposit is paid when signing the agreement, with the remainder paid on moving day. Each month, the tenant is required to electronically transfer rent money to the landlord.

The other type of lease, a lump sum rental, is unique to Korea. A large deposit, typically upwards of 50 percent of the property value, is required when signing the contract. The tenant pays no monthly rent; at the end of the lease, the deposit is returned in full.

Can I see the apartment you just described?

그럼 방금 말한 아파트, 지금 볼 수 있을까요?

geureom banggeum malhan apateu, jigeum bol su isseulkkayo?

Yes, let's go now.

네, 가시죠.

ne, gasijyo.

How old is the building?

건물 지은 지 얼마나 됐나요?

geonmul jieun ji eolmana dwaennayo?

How many bathrooms does the apartment have?

이 아파트에 화장실이 몇 개인가요?

i apateu-e hwajangsiri myeot gaein-gayo?

How much is the monthly building maintenance fee?

관리비는 한 달에 얼마 정도 하죠?

gwallibineun han dare eolma jeongdo hajyo?

I love this apartment. I'd like to sign a contract.

이 집 마음에 드네요. 계약하고 싶어요.

i jip ma-eume deuneyo. gyeyakhago sipeoyo.

I'd like to see some other places.

다른 집도 보고 싶어요.

dareun jipdo bogo sipeoyo.

BANKING & FOREIGN EXCHANGE

bank

은행
eunhaeng

I'd like to open a new account.

계좌를 새로 만들고 싶은데요.
gyejwareul saero mandeulgo sipeundeyo.

Please show me your passport and your alien registration card.

여권이랑 외국인등록증 좀 부탁드려요.
yeokkwonirang oegugindeungnokjeung jom butakdeuryeoyo.

I'd also like to have a debit card made.

그리고 현금카드도 만들고 싶어요.
geurigo hyeongeumkadeudo mandeulgo sipeoyo.

To open a checking or savings account, you will need to present a valid passport with a visa stamp and your Korean alien registration card.

What are your interest rates?

○ 이자율이 얼마죠?

ijayuri eolmajyo?

Do you offer online or mobile banking in English?

○ 영문 인터넷뱅킹이나 모바일뱅킹 되나요?

yeongmun inteonetbaengking-ina mobailbaengking doenayo?

Please issue a digital banking certificate for me.

○ 은행 공인인증서를 발급해 주세요.

eunhaeng gong-ininjeungseoreul balgeupae juseyo.

I'd like to close my bank account.

○ 은행 계좌를 해지하고 싶은데요.

eunhaeng gyejwareul haejihago sipeundeyo.

If you require online or mobile banking, you'll need to request a banking security card and digital banking certificate. A banking security card is a unique card with thirty sets of random integers printed on it. Each set contains a string of four integers. Internet banking sites and mobile banking apps require you to input combinations of these numbers when paying bills and transferring money. Online banking also requires the use of a digital banking certificate and the installation of security software on your PC, cellphone, or tablet. A digital certificate will be issued by your bank and is accessible the first time you log in. It must be kept on every PC or cellphone that you use for internet banking. It can be copied between computers on a USB flash drive or downloaded directly from the banking website. The certificate expires after one year, but can be renewed online.

The security software is automatically installed when you first access the bank website via Internet Explorer. The software is a mixture of anti-virus, anti-spyware, and anti-keylogging tools that will launch every time you access your account online.

foreign exchange(FX) / currency exchange

환전
hwanjeon

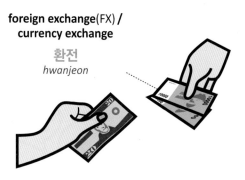

Where can I exchange money?

○ 어디서 환전하나요?
eodiseo hwanjeonhanayo?

Do you handle currency exchange here?

○ 여기서 환전 되나요?
yeogiseo hwanjeon doenayo?

I'd like to change euros to Korean money.

○ 유로화를 한국 돈으로 환전하고 싶은데요.
yurohwareul han-guk don-euro hwanjeonhago sipeundeyo.

A 1 percent commission is charged for cashing traveler's checks.

○ 여행자 수표를 환전하시면 1퍼센트의 수수료가 붙습니다.
yeohaengja supyoreul hwanjeonhasimyeon ilpeosenteu-ui susuryoga butseumnida.

Are foreign transaction fees charged on this credit card?

○ 이 신용카드는 환전 수수료를 내야 하나요?
i sinyongkadeuneun hwanjeon susuryoreul naeya hanayo?

CREDIT CARDS

issuing a credit card

신용카드 발급
sinyongkadeu balgeup

I would like to apply for a credit card.

○ 신용카드를 만들고 싶은데요.
sinyongkadeureul mandeulgo sipeundeyo.

What are the eligibility requirements for obtaining a credit card?

○ 신용카드 발급 조건이 뭔가요?
sinyongkadeu balgeup jokkeoni mwon-gayo?

I lost my credit card.

○ 제 신용카드를 분실했는데요.
je sinyongkadeureul bunsilhaenneundeyo.

To sign up for a credit card, you'll need proof of employment and income. Bring your valid alien registration card and passport as well.

New and replacement cards are delivered by messenger service to your home or office within a week and require photo verification and a signature upon delivery.

When did you lose it?

언제 분실하셨죠?

eonje bunsilhasyeotjyo?

Around 9 pm last night.

어제 밤 9시경에 분실했습니다.

eoje bam ahopsigyeong-e bunsilhaetseumnida.

I need a replacement card.

카드를 재발급 받고 싶은데요.

kadeureul jaebalgeup batgo sipeundeyo.

What is the interest rate for cash advances?

현금서비스 이자율이 얼마나 되나요?

hyeon-geumseobiseu ijayuri eolmana doenayo?

What's the fee for a 12-month installment plan?

12개월 할부 수수료율이 얼마나 되나요?

sibigaewol halbu susuryoyuri eolmana doenayo?

Can I receive a monthly statement in English?

신용카드 사용내역서를 영어로 받을 수 있나요?

sinyongkadeu sayongnaeyeokseoreul yeong-eoro badeul su innayo?

KEB offers an Expat Card that provides numerous benefits, including a 24/7/365 phone help line, website services, and monthly statements all in English. The annual fee is 120,000 won. (Visit http://www.keb.co.kr for details.) Citibank Korea offers similar English-language services and benefits; it also carries an annual fee of 120,000 won. (See http://citibank.co.kr for more information.)

Local cards such as the Samsung Card have lower annual fees but are limited in terms of English-language services.

Would you like to pay in full?

○ 일시불로 하시겠습니까?
ilsibullo hasigetseumnikka?

I'd like to pay for this in three interest-free installments.

○ 무이자 3개월 할부로 해주세요.
muija samgaewol halburo haejuseyo.

I'd like to receive a discount for using this credit card.

○ 이 신용카드로 할인을 받고 싶은데요.
i sinyongkadeuro harineul batgo sipeundeyo.

Is the discount given at the time of purchase or on the statement closing date?

○ 현장할인이 되나요, 아니면 청구할인이 되나요?
hyeonjangharini doenayo, animyeon cheongguharini doenayo?

Common types of credit card discount programs include ones for gas, restaurants and tourist destinations, and shopping. There are also cards that offer discounts for educational programs and English examinations. While discounts may be applied at the time of purchase, some are applied on your statement closing date and appear as deductions on your monthly statement. The number of times you can receive discounts by using your credit card is limited. Large shops and chain restaurants can tell if you qualify for a discount by swiping your card.

In the past, credit cards were available without annual fees. Today, most credit card companies charge an annual fee. Basic credit cards have fees starting at 5,000 won. Cards with more functions have higher fees.

SIGNING UP FOR A CELLPHONE

cellphone shop

핸드폰 대리점
haendeupon daerijeom

I would like to buy a cellphone.

○ 핸드폰을 사고 싶은데요.
haendeuponeul sago sipeundeyo.

Are you a foreigner? If so, we'll need to see an alien registration card or
passport.

○ 외국인이신가요? 외국인이시면 외국인 등록증이나 여권이 필요합니다.
oeguginisin-gayo? oeguginisimyeon oegugin deungnokjeungina yeokkwoni piryohamnida.

I'd like to purchase a smartphone.

○ 저는 스마트폰을 구입하고 싶어요.
jeo-neun seumateuponeul gu-ipago sipeoyo.

Do you want to set up a pre-paid or a monthly plan?

○ 선불제 요금과 후불제 요금이 있는데 어떤 것으로 하시겠어요?
seonbulje yogeumgwa hubulje yogeumi inneunde eotteon geoseuro hasigesseoyo?

I'd like to set up a monthly plan?

○ 후불제 부탁드려요.
hubuljero butakdeuryeoyo.

When you buy a cellphone, you can receive a large discount if you sign a contract.

○ 핸드폰을 구입하실 땐 사용기간 약정을 하시면 기기대금이 많이 할인 됩니다.
haendeuponeul gu-ipasil ttaen sayonggigan yakjeong-eul hasimyeon gigidaegeumi mani harindoemnida.

What is the contract period? / How long is the contract?

○ 계약기간이 얼마나 되죠?
gyeyakgigani eolmana doejyo?

The phone is free if you sign a two-year contract for 50,000 won per month.

○ 요금제 월 50,000원으로 2년 약정을 하시면, 기기 가격이 무료입니다.
yogeumje wol oman won-euro inyeon yakjeong-eul hasimyeon, gigi gagyeogi muryoimnida.

In addition to purchased cellphones, prepaid and rental phones are also available. Rental phones are offered at large hotels and airports.

An alien registration card and passport are required to set up a cellphone contract. Most phones require two- to three-year agreements, and so the handsets are provided at a reduced cost (subsidized price). Activation charges may also apply for new accounts.

Signing a contract for a more expensive plan with a larger number of minutes reduces the overall cost of the hardware. Additionally, that cost is broken up over the period of the contract and a portion is charged in each month's bill. The carriers typically mandate this, and will even charge a small finance fee for this "service."

Korean carriers bill outgoing calls at a fixed per-minute rate regardless of the time of day (no peak/off-peak/free weekends). But the good news is that all incoming calls are free, and there are no roaming charges anywhere within Korea.

TYPES OF HOUSES

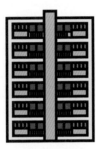

apartment
아파트
apateu

Korean apartments are purchased or rented. Apartment buildings tend to be tall, with upwards of 10 floors. A monthly maintenance fee is added to the rent to cover security, common area cleaning, and other amenities.

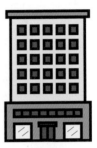

officetel
오피스텔
opiseutel

Officetels are studio apartments that are also zoned as office space. They normally measure between 10 and 20 *pyeong* (33.3 to 66.6 m^2). Supermarkets, restaurants, fitness centers, and other amenities occupy the ground or basement floors.

villa
빌라
billa

Small apartment complexes with less than five floors per building. Due to their smaller size, the security office, waste disposal, and parking are more accessible than at a large apartment complex.

detached home
단독 주택
dandok jutaek

Located inside or outside of cities and featuring small yards or gardens, detached homes are typically one or two stories in height and built with a tall wall that provides privacy and security.

RENTING A HOUSE

real estate agent /
realtor

부동산 중개사
budongsan junggaesa

security deposit

보증금
bojeunggeum

monthly fee rental

월세
wolse

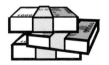

lump sum rental

전세
jeonse

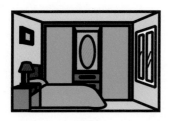

room
방
bang

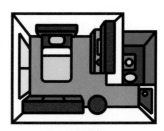

studio
원룸
wollum

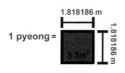

pyeong
(unit of measurement)
평
pyeong

utility bill
공과금
gonggwageum

maintenance fee
관리비
gwallibi

security office
경비실
gyeongbisil

BANKING AND FOREIGN EXCHANGE

rate
이자율
ijayul

digital banking certificate
은행 공인인증서
eunhaeng gong-in-injeungseo

bank security card
은행 보안카드
eunhaeng boankadeu

**foreign exchange(FX) /
currency exchange**
환전
hwanjeon

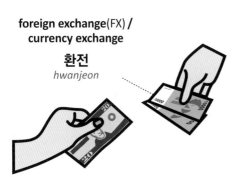

foreign exchange rate
환율
hwanyul

CREDIT CARD

installment plan

할부
halbu

lump sum payment

일시불
ilsibul

credit card discount partners

제휴사
jehyusa

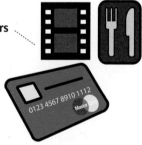

discount on statement closing date

청구할인
cheongguharin

discount at time of purchase

현장할인
hyeonjangharin

CELLPHONES

smartphone
스마트폰
seumateupon

USIM card
유심 카드
yusim kadeu

cell phone wall charger
휴대폰 충전기
hyudaepon chungjeon-gi

plan
요금제
yogeumje

contract / agreement
약정
yakjeong

termination fee
위약금
wiyakgeum

UTILITY PAYMENTS

category
분류
bullyu

bill notification
(for processing)
수납통지서
sunaptongjiseo

payment amount
납부금액
napbugeumaek

standard OCR format
표준 OCR
pyojun ossial

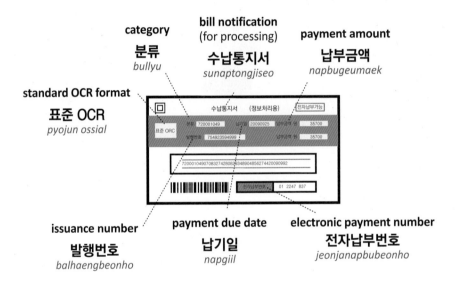

issuance number
발행번호
balhaengbeonho

payment due date
납기일
napgiil

electronic payment number
전자납부번호
jeonjanapbubeonho

There are numerous ways to pay your bills. Utility bills can be paid at post offices, banks, and convenience stores. Some of these locations use an automated bill pay machine or ATM (usually in Korean only).

An online banking account may also be used to transfer money to one of the banks listed on the utility bill. Multiple banks are available so that you can avoid paying internet banking fees. Bank-to-bank transfers may be limited to weekdays between 8 am and 10 pm.

giro request form
(for bank)

지로의뢰서
(수납은행용)
jirouiroeseo
(sunabeunhaengyong)

giro notification
(for account record)

지로통지서(금융결제원용)
jirotongjiseo
(geumnyunggyeoljewonnyong)

giro receipt (for customer)

지로영수증(고객용)
jiroyeongsujeung(gogaegyong)

name

성명
seongmyeong

number

번호
beonho

address

주소
juso

giro number

지로번호
jirobeonho

customer reference number

고객조회번호
gogaekjohoebeonho

payment amount

금액
geumaek

period

월분
wolbun

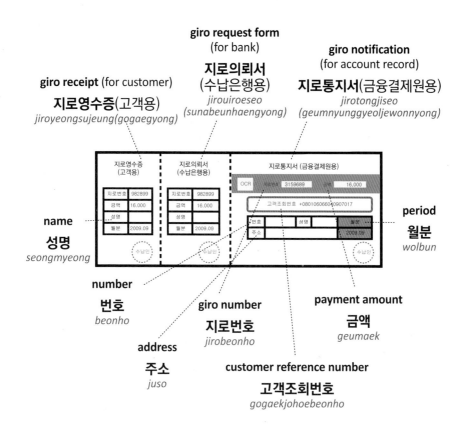

A giro is a direct transfer from the remitter to the payee using a local banking institution. Giro is a common form of payment for utility bills. The modern giro payment was created by European post offices. The US never adopted use of the giro, since payments were traditionally made with paper checks. However, paper checks require a lengthy delivery and processing path before becoming accessible to the payee. The giro payment system eliminates this cumbersome process.

Korean bills have no grace period beyond the due date, and a 2 percent fee is typically assessed for late payments.

GOSIWON

gosiwon

고시원

gosiwon

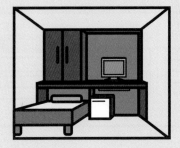

Gosiwon translates to "a place for studying for a state exam." These study rooms were originally designed as quiet getaways for students and others preparing for the intensive civil servant exams.

These days, low-cost dorm-style (single room) *gosiwons* attract migrant workers, and everyday office workers looking to save some money. They do not require the large deposits often associated with apartments. *Jeonse*-type rent is possible, as is month-to-month rent.

A typical *gosiwon* building has around 50 rooms ranging from 2.5 to 3.5 square meters in size. Often, they are built near busy subways stations or university campuses. They include a bed, desk, closet, and internet connection, and sometimes come with A C or a TV. Monthly rent is normally between 200,000 and 400,000 won. Bathrooms and kitchens are shared by floor tenants. Laundry, kimchi, and rice are often free. In Seoul, you can find more than 3,400 *gosiwons* offering units for rent. Some are very vulnerable to fire and burglar.

Gosiwon is an inexpensive option for English teachers seeking to store their belongings while travelling around Korea or going abroad for a month or more.

PHRASES FOR GOSIWON

A *gosiwon* is a low-cost single-room apartment.

⚪ 고시원은 가격이 낮은 원룸이에요.
gosiwoneun gagyeogi najeun wollumieyo.

Do I need to pay key money / a deposit?

⚪ 보증금을 내야 하나요?
bojeunggeumeul naeya hanayo?

What amenities do you offer?

⚪ 어떤 편의 시설이 있나요?
eotteon pyeonui siseori innayo?

Single people often live in a *gosiwon*.

⚪ 많은 싱글들이 고시원에 살아요.
maneun singgeuldeuri gosiwone sarayo.

ENTERTAINMENT &
L E I S U R E

6 ENTERTAINMENT & LEISURE

OVERVIEW Five Things to Do Before Leaving Korea

skate
홍어
hongeo

kimchi
김치
gimchi

makgeolli
막걸리
makgeolli

fermented soybean paste stew
청국장
cheonggukjang

Tasting Fermented Skate, Kimchi, and Makgeolli

There are many different kinds of fermented foods in Korea. These dishes and drinks not only taste great but are also an excellent source of nutrition. Kimchi and the traditional Korean alcohol *makgeolli* are two well-known examples. A unique and somewhat unknown food to foreigners is fermented skate. Fermented skate have an especially pungent smell that may not sit well with some people. Those with weaker stomachs would be better off going with the tofu.

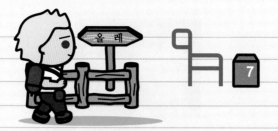

Hiking Jeju's Olle Trails

Jeju Island is one of Korea's most beautiful settings. A pilgrim who walked the road to Santiago de Compostela in Spain developed these hiking paths for a jewel of the island boasting mountains, wind, and sea. Hikers travel its paths all year round— some have called the experience life-changing. Take in the beauty, people, and cuisine of Korea at a leisurely pace on these trails.

Seeing the Sun Rise over a Sea of Clouds from Mt. Seorak's Daecheongbong Peak

At 1,708 meters, Mt. Seorak is the third highest peak in South Korea after Mt. Halla and Mt. Jiri. Associated with the sacred and sublime, it's famous for its beautiful rocks, autumn leaves, and changes with the seasons. Visit its highest summit, Daecheongbong Peak, for the sunrise after a rain and you will encounter a spectacle of low-lying clouds hovering over a golden waterfall in the sunshine. Not to be missed by anyone who likes mountains and the sunrise.

Watching a Shaman Perform a Gut Ceremony

The *gut* was traditionally a kind of festival and ceremony where ordinary shamans consoled wronged spirits or asked for the mercy of the gods. Bringing together traditional music, dance, and culture, it's worth seeing for its beauty and overwhelming atmosphere alone. And with the tremendous energy of the shamans, people are said to find their spirits healed after watching the ceremony. Experience the energy of the shamans firsthand.

Staying Up Drinking with Koreans

Koreans are famous for their love of drinking, singing, and having fun. Why not join some friends for a night of snacks, drinks, life stories, songs, and an all-around good time? Even the most uncomfortable relationship can become close after nights like these.

MOVIES & PERFORMANCES

movie theater

극장
geukjang

Would you like to go see a movie with me?

○ 나랑 영화 보러 갈래요?
narang yeonghwa boreo gallaeyo?

What kind of movies do you like?

○ 어떤 영화를 좋아해요?
eotteon yeonghwareul joahaeyo?

I like science fiction movies.

○ SF 영화를 좋아해요.
eseu-epeu yeonghwareul joahaeyo.

How about *The Dark Knight Rises*?

이번에 새로 나오는 '다크 나이트 라이즈' 어때요?

ibeone saero naoneun dakeu naiteu raijeu eottaeyo?

Does it have English subtitles?

영어자막이 있나요?

yeong-eojamagi innayo?

No, it's in English with Korean subtitles.

아니요. 영어로 대사가 나오고, 한국어 자막이 있어요.

aniyo. yeong-eoro daesaga naogo, han-gugeo jamagi isseoyo.

Great. Let's go to see that movie.

좋아요. 우리 그 영화 보러 가요.

joayo. uri geu yeonghwa boreo gayo.

I'd like tickets for two adults to see *The Dark Knight Rises* at 7:50 pm.

'다크 나이트 라이즈' 7시 50분 거, 어른 두 사람이요.

dakeu naiteu raijeu ilgopsi osipbun geo, eoreun du saramiyo.

Where would you like to sit in the theater?

어느 좌석으로 드릴까요?

eoneu jwaseogeuro deurilkkayo?

I'd like an aisle seat that's not too close to the screen.

약간 뒤쪽 통로 쪽으로 주세요.

yakgan dwijjok tongno jjogeuro juseyo.

Row G, Seats 1 and 2.

고객님, G열, 1, 2번 좌석입니다.

gogaengnim, jiyeol, il, ibeon jwaseogimnida.

I saw a movie called *Children of Men* last week.

◌ 지난 주에 '칠드런 오브 맨'이라는 영화 봤어요.
  jinan ju-e childeureonobeumaeniraneun yeonghwa bwasseoyo.

Did you like that movie?

◌ 그 영화 좋았어요?
  geu yeonghwa joasseoyo?

Yes, it was really powerful.

◌ 네, 완전히 감동적이었어요.
  ne, wanjeonhi gamdongjeogieosseoyo.

Which musical is popular these days?

◌ 요즘 뮤지컬 뭐가 재미있죠?
  yojeum myujikeol mwoga jaemiitjyo?

Going to the movies is a popular pastime, so it's best to make a reservation ahead of time. You can purchase tickets on the theater's website or at the box office. Many theaters have automated kiosks to handle ticketing.

Your seat is assigned when you buy your ticket. Real-time seating charts are available online or at the box office. As you might guess, the middle seats are the first to sell out.

Online reservations have no hidden service fees. However, full payment for the tickets must be made at the time of the reservation. Many Korean credit cards and point cards can score you a discount on movie tickets. Visit the theater website or box office for a complete listing of acceptable cards.

theater

공연장
gong-yeonjang

Jekyll and Hyde has been popular recently.

요즘, '지킬 앤 하이드'라는 뮤지컬이 재미있대요.
yojeum, jikiraenhaideuraneun myujikeori jaemiitdaeyo.

Would you like to go see it with me tomorrow?

내일 같이 보러 가시겠어요?
naeil gachi boreo gasigesseoyo?

That sounds great.

좋아요.
joayo.

Thanks, I had a great time.

덕분에 정말 재미있는 공연을 봤습니다.
deokbune jeongmal jaemiinneun gong-yeoneul bwatseumnida.

SINGING ROOMS

singing room

노래방
noraebang

Are there any rooms available here?
- 방 있어요?
  bang isseoyo?

How many people are in your party?
- 몇 분이세요?
  myeot buniseyo?

There are eight of us. Do you have any large rooms?
- 8명이요. 큰 방 있어요?
  yeodeolmyeong-iyo. keun bang isseoyo?

How much is it per hour?
- 한 시간에 얼마인가요?
  han sigane eolmain-gayo?

Could you pass me the songbook?

선곡집 좀 주시겠어요?
seon-gokjip jom jusigesseoyo?

Can you give us some extra time for free?

서비스로 시간을 좀 더 주실 수 있나요?
seobiseuro siganeul jom deo jusil su innayo?

Do you know this song?

이 노래 아세요?
i norae aseyo?

Let's sing it together.

우리 같이 노래 불러요.
uri gachi norae bulleoyo.

Why don't you sing first?

먼저 노래 하세요.
meonjeo norae haseyo.

Can you help me find the song "_____" by_____?

_____의 노래 "_____" 찾는 것 좀 도와주시겠어요?
_____ui norae _____ channeun geot jom dowajusigesseoyo?

Time's up.

시간이 다 됐어요.
sigani da dwaesseoyo.

We'd like to add another hour.

한 시간만 연장해주세요.
han siganman yeonjanghaejuseyo.

GOING FOR DRINKS & DRINKING ETIQUETTE

drinking culture

음주문화
uemjumunhwa

Would you like to have a drink with me sometime?

우리 언제 술이나 같이 할까요?
uri eonje surina gachi halkkayo?

That sounds good. Let me know when you're free.

네. 좋아요. 시간 괜찮을 때 같이 한번 마셔요.
ne. joayo. sigan gwaenchaneul ttae gachi hanbeon masyeoyo.

Do you have time tonight?

오늘 저녁에 시간 있으세요?
oneul jeonyeoge sigan isseuseyo?

Yes, I do.

네. 괜찮습니다.
ne. gwaenchansseumnida.

Would you like to go out for a cold beer?

◌ 그럼 우리 시원하게 맥주 한잔하러 갈까요?
geureom uri siwonhage maekju hanjanhareo galkkayo?

Let's go have a drink together.

◌ 오늘 술 한잔하러 가요.
oneul sul hanjanhareo gayo.

What food (snacks) would you like to order?

◌ 안주로는 뭐가 좋으세요?
anjuroneun mwoga joeuseyo?

Today, I'd like to drink in the traditional Korean style.

◌ 오늘은 한국적인 분위기에서 술을 마셔보고 싶어요.
oneureun han-gukjeogin bunwigieseo sureul masyeobogo sipeoyo.

How about *makgeolli* and kimchi pancakes?

◌ 그럼 막걸리에 김치전 어떠세요?
geureom makgeollie gimchijeon eotteoseyo?

That's great!

◌ 너무 좋아요!
neomu joayo!

How much can you drink? / How high is your alcohol tolerance?

◌ 주량은 어느 정도 되세요?
juryang-eun eoneu jeongdo doeseyo?

I can drink three bottles of beer.

◌ 맥주 세 병 정도 마셔요.
maekju se byeong jeongdo masyeoyo.

What types of drinks do you like?

○ 어떤 술을 좋아하세요?
eotteon sureul joahaseyo?

My favorite drink is *baekseju* ("hundred-year wine"), but I also like Andong soju.

○ 백세주를 제일 좋아하고, 안동소주도 좋아해요.
baeksejureul jeil joahago, andongsojudo joahaeyo.

Cheers!

○ 건배!
geonbae!

Bottoms up!

○ 원샷!
wonsyat!

Business deals are often done over drinks—you may find yourself going out with coworkers and customers each week. Sharing drinks is a way of removing inhibitions and showing your true character. Follow these rules to show respect, build friendships, and earn the trust of others.

If you're out with the intention of only eating, have at least one drink. Koreans consider this to be a time for bonding, and an early refusal to drink will be considered bad manners. If you do not want to drink more than that, make it known before the event starts, as Koreans may relax the rules for foreigners. Otherwise, drink slowly, keeping your glass partially full as long as possible and thus postponing a refill. Don't drive drunk. There are plenty of ways to travel home safely, including public transportation, a taxi, or a proxy driver.

Hold your glass with both hands when you are being served. Always lead with your right hand regardless of your handedness. When your neighbors' glasses are completely empty, serve them using both hands. Your right hand should always be the leading arm. Never fill your own glass—those around you should be taking care of you. Someone will notice sooner or later and assist you.

I'm not feeling good today, so I'm going to drink slowly.

○ 제가 오늘은 몸이 좀 안 좋아서, 천천히 마실게요.
jega oneureun momi jom an joaseo, cheoncheonhi masilkkeyo.

Where should we go for the second round?

○ 2차는 어디로 갈까요?
ichaneun eodiro galkkayo?

There's a popular club around Hongik University. Do you want to go there?

○ 홍대 앞에 좋은 클럽이 있는데 거기로 갈까요?
hongdae ape jo-eun keulleobi inneunde geogiro galkkayo?

I have a hangover today.

○ 오늘 숙취가 있어요.
oneul sukchwiga isseoyo.

I completely blacked out last night.

○ 어젯밤 필름이 끊겼어요.
eojetbam pilleumi kkeunkyeosseoyo.

Korean culture is accepting of drunken behavior, for good or bad. Frank conversation is part of the evening's agenda, so don't be surprised to hear intense feelings being expressed. Conversations flow with an honesty and directness that's not normally tolerated between a subordinate and their manager in the office. This is one of the few times a worker can express their true opinion to everyone. And when things get a little out of hand, a forgive-and-forget attitude seems to follow a night on the town.

GYMS

gym
헬스클럽
helseukeulleop

How much does a monthly membership cost?

○ 헬스클럽 이용 요금이 한 달에 얼마인가요?
helseukeulleop iyong yogeumi han dare eolmain-gayo?

Do you offer a one-day trial membership?

○ 시험삼아 하루만 운동해볼 수 있어요?
siheomsama haruman undonghaebol su isseoyo?

I'd like to sign up for a membership.

○ 회원으로 등록하고 싶은데요.
hoewoneuro deungnokhago sipeundeyo.

What type of equipment do you have?

○ 어떤 시설이 있나요?
eotteon siseori innayo?

Do you have a pool?

○ 수영장이 있나요?
suyeongjangi innayo?

What are your hours of operation?

○ 영업시간이 어떻게 되나요?
yeong-eopsigani eotteoke doenayo?

What kinds of classes do you offer?

○ 어떤 강습이 있나요?
eotteon gangseubi innayo?

Please show me how to use this machine.

○ 이 운동기구 어떻게 사용하는지 알려주세요.
i undonggigu eotteoke sayonghaneunji allyeojuseyo.

How much is a personal trainer?

○ 개인 트레이너에게 레슨을 받으면 얼마인가요?
gaein teureineo-ege reseuneul badeumyeon eolmain-gayo?

What should I bring with me to the gym?

○ 클럽 이용 시 필요한 준비물은 무엇인가요?
keulleop iyong si piryohan junbimureun mueosin-gayo?

TAKING A VACATION

summer vacation

여름휴가
yeoreumhyuga

When will you take your summer vacation?

◯ 여름휴가 언제 가세요?
yeoreumhyuga eonje gaseyo?

Where will you go?

◯ 어디로 가나요?
eodiro ganayo?

I'm going to the East Sea.

◯ 동해 바다로 가요.
donghae badaro gayo.

I'll just stay home.

◯ 집에 있을 거예요.
jibe isseul geoyeyo.

Can you recommend a good holiday destination?

◌ 좋은 휴가지 좀 추천해 주시겠어요?
jo-eun hyugaji jom chucheonhae jusigesseoyo?

How long is your vacation?

◌ 휴가 며칠 가요?
hyuga myeochil gayo?

I have 4 days off.

◌ 4일 동안 쉬어요.
sail dongan swieoyo.

Did you make a hotel reservation?

◌ 숙소는 예약했나요?
suksoneun yeyakhaennayo?

I made a reservation at a nice hotel with a seaside view.

◌ 네, 바닷가 전망 좋은 호텔 예약해 놨어요.
ne, badatga jeonmang jo-eun hotel yeyakhae nwasseoyo.

To keep businesses running smoothly year round, most Korean companies specify a time period when employees should take their summer vacation. Normally this falls within the month of August. people usually take a week off.

ski

스키
seuki

Let's go skiing this weekend.

이번 주말에 스키 타러 가요.
ibeon jumare seuki tareo gayo.

Do you have your own skis?

스키를 가지고 있나요?
seukireul gajigo innayo?

I need to rent skis.

스키를 빌려야 되요.
seukireul billyeoya doeyo.

The local ski season begins in late November and normally extends through March. Many provinces are known for their resorts. Gangwon-do province and Gyeonggi-do province are among the better-known places for large ski resorts.

hiking

등산
deungsan

Let's hike Mt. Seorak this weekend.

○ 이번 주말에 설악산에 등산 가요.
ibeon jumare seoraksane deungsan gayo.

This mountain is good for hiking.

○ 이 산은 등산하기 좋은 곳이에요.
i san-eun deungsanhagi jo-eun gosieyo.

Nearly 80 percent of the Korean Peninsula is covered in mountains. And there are also 20 National Parks throughout the country. It's only natural, then, that hiking would become a popular sport here. It's not uncommon for companies to subsidize employee outdoor clubs.

Most hiking trails are free or cost just a few thousand won for admission and parking. Koreans carry a wealth of snacks in their backpack including *gimbap* (seaweed-wrapped rice rolls), small sausages, oranges, bananas, or other fruit. After your hike, you'll find an assortment of restaurants near the park entrance to satisfy any lingering hunger.

TOURS

tour

여행
yeohaeng

I'm interested in traveling to _____.

○ _____로 여행가고 싶은데요.
_____*ro yeohaeng-gago sipeundeyo.*

Do you have a three-day, two-night package tour for Busan?

○ 부산까지 가는 2박 3일 숙박 포함된 패키지여행 상품이 있나요?
busankkaji ganeun ibak samil sukbak pohamdoen paekijiyeohaeng sangpumi innayo?

How much is it?

○ 얼마나 하나요?
eolmana hanayo?

Do you offer any discounts?

○ 할인을 좀 해주실 수 있나요?
harineul jom haejusil su innayo?

Are transportation, accommodations, meals, and other expenses all included in the price?

○ 교통, 숙박, 식사 등 모든 비용이 포함된 가격인가요?

gyotong, sukbak, siksa deung modeun biyongi pohamdoen gagyeogin-gayo?

Transportation and accommodations are included, but the meals only include breakfast.

○ 교통과 숙박은 포함되어 있고, 식사는 조식만 포함되어 있습니다.

gyotonggwa sukbageun pohamdoe-eo itgo, siksaneun josingman pohamdoe-eo itseumnida.

Is there an English-speaking tour guide?

○ 영어 하는 가이드가 있나요?

yeong-eo haneun gaideuga innayo?

I would like to make a reservation for two people.

○ 두 사람 예약하고 싶어요.

du saram yeyakhago sipeoyo

How should I dress?

○ 옷은 어떻게 입어야 하나요?

oseun eotteoke ibeoya hanayo?

In addition to one-day tours for $50 to $60, a free six-hour transit tour to Seoul's Myeongdong neighborhood is offered. The bus departs from Incheon Airport at 9 am and returns at 3 pm. Go to the Hana Tour Desk at the first floor Arrival Hall between Gates 8 and 9. (+82-2-743-6605, http://www.hanatourintl.com).

For more information, contact the Korea Tourism Organization (+82-2-1330, http://www.visitkorea.or.kr).

Where are we leaving from?

어디에서 출발하죠?

eodieseo chulbalhajyo?

What time should we meet?

몇 시에 만나요?

myeot sie mannayo ?

What time do we arrive in Busan?

몇 시에 부산에 도착하지요?

myeot sie busane dochakhajiyo?

Is there any pick-up service?

픽업 서비스는 없나요?

pigeop seobiseuneun eomnayo?

MOVIE THEATERS

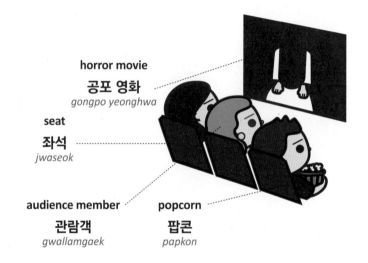

horror movie
공포 영화
gongpo yeonghwa

seat
좌석
jwaseok

audience member
관람객
gwallamgaek

popcorn
팝콘
papkon

science fiction
공상 과학
gongsang gwahak

comedy
코메디
komedi

action
액션
aeksyeon

row G, seat 2
G열 2번 좌석
jiyeol ibeon jwaseok

discount
할인
harin

seating chart
좌석 배치도
jwaseok baechido

SINGING ROOMS

karaoke machine
노래방 기계
noraebang gigye

remote control
리모콘
rimokon

tambourine
탬버린
taembeorin

microphone
마이크
maikeu

songbook
노래방 선곡집
noraebang seon-gokjip

GYMS

bench press
벤치 프레스
benchi peureseu

exercise bike
운동용 자전거
undong-yong jajeon-g

gym
헬스클럽
helseukeulleop

treadmill
러닝머신
reoningmeosin

exercise mat
운동용 매트
undong-yong maeteu

punching bag
샌드백
saendeubaek

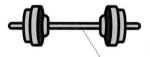

barbell
역기
yeokgi

dumbbells / weights
아령
aryeong

personal trainer
개인 트레이너
gaein teureineo

sit-ups
윗몸 일으키기
winmom ireukigi

push-ups
팔굽혀 펴기
palgupyeo pyeogi

yoga
요가
yoga

aerobics
에어로빅
e-eorobik

dance
춤
chum

Pilates
필라테스
pillateseu

VACATION

inner tube
튜브
tyubeu

water park
물놀이공원
mulnorigong-won

beach
바닷가
badatga

mountain
산
san

island
섬
seom

outdoor hot spring

노천탕
nocheontang

hot spring

온천
oncheon

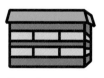

timeshare condo

콘도
kondo

pension

펜션
pensyeon

HIKING

hiking
등산
deungsan

sunglasses
선글라스
seon-geulaseu

summit
정상
jeongsang

backpack
등산용 배낭
deungsanyong baenang

walking stick
등산용 스틱
deungsanyong seutik

hiking boots
등산화
deungsanhwa

WINTER SPORTS

ice skate
스케이트
seukeiteu

snowboard
스노보드
seunobodeu

ski lift
스키 리프트
seuki ripeuteu

ski poles
스키 폴
seuki pol

ski boots
스키 부츠
seuki bucheu

ski
스키
seuki

LIQUOR

soju
소주
soju

The most popular Korean Korean alcoholic drink. With an alcohol content ranging from 20 to 40 percent, it's clear and distilled from rice, tapioca, potato, barley, or wheat. Soju is popular because it's inexpensive, widely available, and yields seven shots per 330 ml glass bottle.

makgeolli
막걸리
makgeolli

Alcohol content 6 percent. Can be purchased in supermarkets and at neighborhood convenience stores in large 1.2-liter plastic bottles. Normally milky white in color, it's made from fermented rice, yeast, and water. In restaurants, it's commonly served in ceramic bowls (also 1.2 liters) using a ladle.

Andong soju
안동 소주
andong soju

Alcohol content 45 percent. Made from steamed rice and malted wheat. Government-regulated, it's brewed in the city of Andong in Gyeongsangbuk-do province. It's considered a premium soju.

Baekseju
백세주
baekseju

Literally meaning "hundred-year wine," this is a light earthy rice wine with ginseng and eleven other Oriental herbs.

boilermaker ("Bomb Drink")
폭탄주
poktanju

A shot of soju or whiskey is dropped into a large glass of Korean beer, which is drunk all at once. Similar to a Western boilermaker, where a shot of whiskey is dropped into a glass of beer.

soju cocktails
소주 칵테일
soju kakteil

Milder and sweeter than straight soju, these cocktails are becoming popular outside of Korea at soju cocktail bars. Common flavors include lemon, mango, grape, pineapple, melon, peach, and yogurt. Lemon-lime soda is normally added to make the drink bubbly. If fruit is used, the pulp is always blended with the soju and served in a pitcher. Soju cocktails are not found in typical Korean bars, so you'll need to do some research to find them.

wine
와인
wain

bottled beer
병맥주
byeongmaekju

draft beer
생맥주
saengmaekju

cocktails
칵테일
kakteil

PUBLIC BATHS & JJIMJILBANGS

public bathhouse
목욕탕
mogyoktang

hot water bath
온탕
ontang

scrubbing towel
때수건
ttaesugeon

professional scrubber
때밀이
ttaemiri

Public baths are commonly found in busy neighborhoods, hotels, and business districts. They're open during the day and do not offer the sleeping areas or other recreational services that are found in a *jjimjilbang*. Men and women are separated after entering the facility—there are no common areas for both sexes. Public baths offer body scrubs, facials, and body massages. Body scrubs are a healthy method of skin exfoliation. By removing the upper layer of dead skin cells, you can unclog your pores and help healthy new layers of skin develop.

PHRASES FOR THE BATHHOUSE

I'd like a body scrub.
○ 때를 밀고 싶은데요.
ttaereul milgo sipeundeyo.

Please do it more gently.
○ 약하게 해주세요.
yakhage haejuseyo.

jimjilbang
찜질방
jjimjilbang

yellow earth sauna
황토 불가마
hwangto bulgama

charcoal sauna
참숯 불가마
chamsut bulgama

spa clothing
찜질복
jjimjilbok

forest room
삼림욕방
sallimyokbang

napping
잠자기
jamjagi

sweet rice drink
식혜
sikhye

oven-roasted eggs
구운 달걀
guun dalgyal

pillow
베개
begae

Jjimjilbang are inexpensive places for businessmen, couples, and families to relax and relieve stress. The cost is normally around 10,000 won per person. Amenities include showers, steam rooms, hot tubs, massages (extra fee), sleeping areas with heated floors, snack rooms (snacks cost extra), internet-connected computer rooms, and large-screen televisions. They're open 24 hours a day, 365 days per year. If you're out late and don't feel like taking a taxi home, consider spending the night relaxing at a *jjimjilbang*.

SHOPPING

7 SHOPPING

OVERVIEW Types of Shops & Basic Expressions

Koreans love to shop. Korea's post-war economic boom sparked a consumer culture second-to-none, especially in big cities like Seoul, where you'll find grand department stores, cavernous shopping malls, high-end luxury shops, traditional outdoor markets, supermarkets, hole-in-the-wall shops and a myriad of other places eager to relieve you of your shopping dollars.

   Perhaps unsurprisingly, Seoul is the best place to shop offering Korea's largest collection of department stores with the widest selection of goods. Busan earns a special mention since it's home to the world's largest department store, the gargantuan Shinsegae Centum City. Korean retail culture accommodates shoppers of all budgets.

department store
백화점
baekhwajeom

supermarket
슈퍼마켓
syupeomaket

convenience store
편의점
pyeonuijeom

bakery

빵집

ppangjip

electronics store

전자상가

jeonjasangga

bookstore

서점

seojeom

butcher

정육점

Jeong-yukjeom

hardware store

철물점

cheolmuljeom

furniture shop

가구점

gagujeom

liquor store

주류 판매점

juryu panmaejeom

flower shop

꽃집

kkotjip

stationery shop

문구점

mungujeom

Where can I buy a _____?

◌ _____은/는 어디에서 살 수 있나요?
   _____eun/neun eodieseo sal su innayo?

You can get that at a _____ .

◌ _____에서 살 수 있어요.
   _____eseo sal su isseoyo.

I'm going to the _____ .

◌ _____에 갈 거예요.
   _____e gal geoyeyo.

Can you recommend a good _____ (place)?

◌ 좋은 _____ 좀 알려주세요.
   Jo-eun _____ jom allyeojuseyo.

Is there a _____ around here?

◌ 근처에 _____이/가 어디 있나요?
   geuncheo-e _____i/ga eodi innayo?

Where's the nearest _____ ?

◌ 제일 가까운 _____은/는 어디죠?
   jeil gakkaun _____eun/neun eodijyo?

SHOPPING

shopping

쇼핑
syoping

I'm looking for _____.

_____ 찾는데요.
_____ *channeundeyo.*

Do you carry _____?

_____ 있나요?
_____ *innayo?*

How can I help you?

무엇을 도와드릴까요?
mueoseul dowadeurilkkayo?

No, thanks.

괜찮아요.
gwaenchanayo.

---

fitting room

탈의실
taruisil

I'm just browsing.

○ 그냥 구경하는 중이에요.
geunyang gugyeonghaneun jung-ieyo.

Can I try this on?

○ 입어볼 수 있나요?
ibeobol su innayo?

Do you have this in a bigger / smaller size?

○ 좀 더 큰 / 작은 사이즈 있나요?
jom deo keun / jageun saijeu innayo?

Do you have a different pattern for this design?

○ 이 디자인으로 다른 무늬가 있나요?
i dijaineuro dareun munuiga innayo?

Do you have it any other colors?

○ 다른 컬러가 있나요?
dareun keolleoga innayo?

I'll think about it.

생각 좀 해볼게요.
saenggak jom haebolkkeyo.

I like it.

이거 마음에 들어요.
igeo maeume deureoyo.

Do you have any more in stock?

물건이 더 있나요?
mulgeoni deo innayo?

Are there any sales going on now?

세일을 하나요?
seireul hanayo?

How much is this?

이거 얼마예요?
igeo eolmayeyo?

Do you offer duty-free shopping?

면세가 가능한가요?
myeonsega ganeunghan-gayo?

When shopping for clothes, note that sizes and cuts are very different than in Western countries. The general trend in Asia is toward tighter-fitting clothes and smaller sizes. Korea has its own shoe sizes, which are measured in millimeters (mm). Look for conversion charts to find your Korean shoe size.

Can you give me a discount?

◌ 좀 깎아 주세요.
jom kkakka juseyo.

Can I use your calculator?

◌ 계산기 좀 쓸 수 있을까요?
gyesan-gi jom sseul su isseulkkayo?

I'll take it.

◌ 이걸로 살게요.
igeollo salgeyo.

Expect to haggle with independent shop stall owners. Each of them keeps a calculator handy. Ask to borrow it and type in the amount you would like to pay. You may end up going back and forth several times before the sale is made. Shopping malls, chain stores, and department stores do not allow haggling.

Korean department stores feature both local and international brands. They hold big sales several times a year, especially around holidays. Sale items typically migrate to a single rack, so look for signs.

Many regular stores offer duty-free items that are tax refundable at the airport. Look for the "Duty Free" sign at the register, or simply ask. After making a purchase, you will receive a special tax refund slip from the shop. Take the slip, the original receipt, and the item as carry-ons. Go to the Tax Refund Counter to receive a stamp verifying the items are leaving the country. Finally, take the papers to a separate nearby Tax Refund payment counter for processing and to receive your refund in US dollars or Korean won.

AT THE CASH REGISTER

cash register

계산대

gyeosandae

Please calculate my bill.

○ 계산 부탁드려요.
gyesan butakdeuryeoyo.

Do you accept credit cards?

○ 신용카드 받습니까?
sinyongkadeu batseumnikka?

Would you like to pay in full or over three months with no interest?

○ 일시불로 하시겠습니까? 무이자 3개월 할부로 하시겠습니까?
ilsibullo hasigetseumnikka? muija samgaewol halburo hasigetseumnikka?

I would like to pay for this in three interest-free installments.

○ 무이자 3개월 할부로 해주세요.
muija samgaewol halburo haejuseyo.

Please sign here.

여기에 서명 좀 해주세요.
yeogie seomyeong jom haejuseyo.

Would you like to earn points or receive a discount?

포인트 적립 해드릴까요, 아니면 할인해드릴까요?
pointeu jeongnip haedeurilkkayo, animyeon harinhaedeurilkkayo?

May I have a receipt, please?

영수증 좀 부탁드려요.
yeongsujeung jom butakdeuryeoyo.

May I have a shopping bag?

쇼핑백 하나 부탁드려요.
syopingbaek hana butakdeuryeoyo.

Do you need a plastic bag?

비닐봉지 필요하세요?
binilbongji piryohaseyo?

Korea's competitive retail and restaurant industry environment has spurred the widespread use of point cards (loyalty cards). By redeeming the points you earn, you can receive store gift certificates, transfer points to airline miles, pay a portion of your bill, or receive numerous other benefits for your store loyalty. Coffee shops, restaurants, bakeries, and ice cream shops also accept point cards. A sign near the register will tell you which cards are accepted and what discounts are given. Credit cards often provide rewards as well. Visit their respective websites for additional information.

return

환불

hwanbul

What is your return policy?

○ 교환 및 환불 규정이 어떻게 되죠?

gyohwan mit hwanbul gyujeong-i eotteoke doejyo?

You can get a refund for up to seven days on unused merchandise with a receipt.

○ 상품의 가격표를 떼지 않고 영수증을 지참하면 7일 이내에 환불이 가능
합니다.

sangpumui gagyeokpyoreul tteji anko yeongsujeungeul jichamhamyeon chiril inae-e hwanburi ganeunghamnida.

Unopened merchandise may be returned for a refund.

○ 미개봉 상품은 반품이 가능합니다.

migaebong sangpumeun banpumi ganeunghamnida.

Can I return this to any store location?

다른 매장에서도 환불 받을 수 있나요?

dareun maejang-eseodo hwanbul badeul su innayo?

The item can only be returned to this location.

이 상품은 이 매장에서만 환불 가능합니다.

i sangpumeun i maejang-eseoman hwanbul ganeunghamnida.

Unworn clothing can be returned within 30 days.

착용하지 않은 옷은 30일 이내에 환불이 가능합니다.

chagyonghaji aneun oseun samsibil inae-e hwanburi ganeunghamnida.

There are no refunds on sale items.

세일 상품은 환불이 불가능합니다.

seil sangpumeun hwanburi bulganeunghamnida.

I would like to exchange this for a bigger size.

이 옷, 한 치수 더 큰 것으로 교환 부탁드려요.

i ot, han chisu deo keun geoseuro gyohwan butakdeuryeoyo.

Sir / Ma'am, that item is not available in your size right now. Would you like to choose something else?

고객님, 이 상품은 요청하신 사이즈가 품절입니다. 다른 상품으로 교환 하시겠습니까?

gogaengnim, i sangpumeun yocheonghasin saijeuga pumjeorimnida. dareun sangpumeuro gyohwanhasigetseumnikka?

Well, first of all, I'd like a full refund.

그럼, 우선 모두 환불해 주세요.

geureom, useon modu hwanbulhae juseyo

exchange

교환

gyohwan

I bought this cup yesterday and would like to exchange it.

이 컵 어제 사간 건데, 다른 컵으로 바꾸고 싶어요.
i keop eoje sagan geonde, dareun keobeuro bakkugo sipeoyo.

Do you have the receipt?

영수증을 가지고 계세요?
yeongsujeung-eul gajigo gyeseyo?

We can give you the difference in cash.

차액은 현금으로 환불해 드리겠습니다.
cha-aegeun hyeongeumeuro hwanbulhae deurigetseumnida.

Could I see your credit card and receipt? I'll cancel the purchase for you.

구매하실 때 사용하신 신용카드와 명세서를 주세요. 구입을 취소해 드리겠습니다.
gumaehasil ttae sayonghasin sinyongkadeuwa myeongseseoreul juseyo. gu-ibeul chwisohae deurigetseumnida.

GENERAL SHOPPING

clothing and fashion

옷

ot

cosmetics

화장품

hwajangpum

jewelry

보석류

boseongnyu

electronics

가전제품

gajeonjepum

CLOTHING

suit
정장
jeongjang

dress
원피스
wonpiseu

T-shirt
티셔츠
tisyeocheu

shirt
남방
nambang

dress shirt
와이셔츠
waisyeocheu

jacket
재킷 / 잠바
jaekit / jamba

sweater
스웨터
seuweteo

coat
코트
koteu

skirt
치마
chima

jeans
청바지
cheongbaji

pants
바지
baji

pajamas
잠옷
jamot

sweatsuit
운동복
undongbok

ACCESSORIES

hat
모자
moja

bag
가방
gabang

tie
넥타이
nektai

scarf
머플러
meopeulleo

silk scarf
스카프
seukapeu

earrings
귀걸이
gwigeori

ring
반지
banji

necklace
목걸이
mokgeori

glasses
안경
an-gyeong

sunglasses
선글라스
seon-geullaseu

belt
벨트
belteu

watch
시계
sigye

socks
양말
yangmal

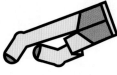

pantyhose
스타킹
seutaking

SHOES

formal shoes
구두
gudu

high heels
하이힐
haihil

flat shoes
단화
danhwa

sandals
샌들
saendeul

flip-flops
조리샌들
jorisaendeul

slippers
슬리퍼
seullipeo

sneakers
운동화
undonghwa

hiking boots
등산화
deungsanhwa

boots
부츠
bucheu

shoe insert
신발 깔창
sinbal kkalchang

GROCERIES

vegetables

야채 / 채소
yachae / chaeso

carrot	cucumber	potato	radish	lettuce	onion	squash
당근	**오이**	**감자**	**무**	**상추**	**양파**	**호박**
danggeun	*oi*	*gamja*	*mu*	*sangchu*	*yangpa*	*hobak*

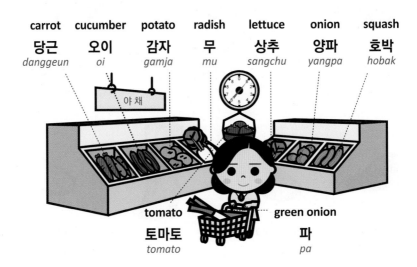

야채

tomato

토마토
tomato

green onion

파
pa

I'd like two kilograms of _____ .

_____2킬로그램만 주세요.
_____ikillogeuraemman juseyo.

Could you please weigh this / these _____ ?

_____무게 좀 달아주시겠어요?
_____muge jom darajusigesseoyo?

chili pepper
고추
gochu

bell pepper
피망 / 파프리카
pimang / papeurika

broccoli
브로콜리
beurokolli

napa cabbage
배추
baechu

garlic
마늘
maneul

eggplant
가지
gaji

fruit

과일
gwail

asian pear

배
bae

strawberry

딸기
ttalgi

banana

바나나
banana

apple

사과
sagwa

korean melon

참외
chamoe

watermelon

수박
subak

persimon

감
gam

meat

정육

jeongyuk

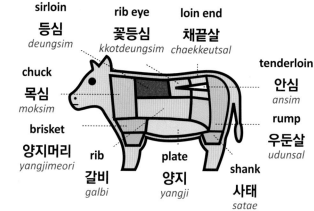

beef

소고기

sogogi

sirloin

등심

deungsim

rib eye

꽃등심

kkotdeungsim

loin end

채끝살

chaekkeutsal

chuck

목심

moksim

tenderloin

안심

ansim

brisket

양지머리

yangjimeori

rump

우둔살

udunsal

rib

갈비

galbi

plate

양지

yangji

shank

사태

satae

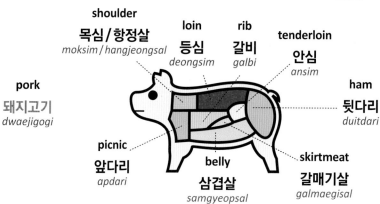

pork

돼지고기

dwaejigogi

shoulder

목심 / 항정살

moksim / hangjeongsal

loin

등심

deongsim

rib

갈비

galbi

tenderloin

안심

ansim

ham

뒷다리

duitdari

picnic

앞다리

apdari

belly

삼겹살

samgyeopsal

skirtmeat

갈매기살

galmaegisal

RECEIPTS

product name
상품명
sangpummyeong

quantity
수량
suryang

price
금액
geumaek

non-taxable amount
면세
myeonse

taxable amount
과세
gwase

tax
부가세
bugase

total
합계
hapgye

영 수 증

상품명	수량	금액

면세	10,000
과세	23,000
부가세	500
합계	33,500

카드종류	해외마스터
승인금액	33.500원 할부 OO개월
카드번호	7578********789
승인번호 ID	12345678

포인트카드

회원번호	1234********567
금회포인트	20
누계포인트	3,220
사용가능포인트	3,220

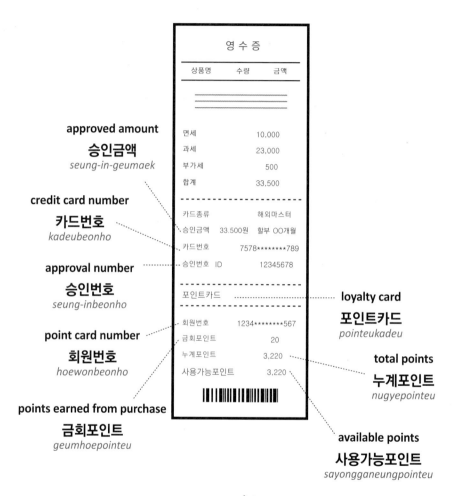

approved amount
승인금액
seung-in-geumaek

credit card number
카드번호
kadeubeonho

approval number
승인번호
seung-inbeonho

point card number
회원번호
hoewonbeonho

points earned from purchase
금회포인트
geumhoepointeu

loyalty card
포인트카드
pointeukadeu

total points
누계포인트
nugyepointeu

available points
사용가능포인트
sayongganeungpointeu

receipt
영수증
yeongsujeung

Receipt content:

영 수 증

상품명　　수량　　금액

면세　　　10.000
과세　　　23.000
부가세　　　500
합계　　　33.500

카드종류　　해외마스터
승인금액　33.500원　할부 OO개월
카드번호　7578********789
승인번호 ID　12345678

포인트카드

회원번호　1234********567
금회포인트　20
누계포인트　3.220
사용가능포인트　3.220

DELIVERY SERVICE

delivery service

택배
taekbae

deliveryman

택배기사
taekbaegisa

Taekbae is a quick, reliable, and inexpensive form of package pickup and delivery service in Korea. Whether you are sending something to a friend, selling something, or doing business, *taekbae* is the way to go.

The deliveryman will pick up packages from your home or office, or even a nearby convenience store, at no extra charge. Make sure you get a copy of the delivery document as proof of receipt. You'll also find a tracking number listed there. Deliveries within Korea take up to one or two days. You can even use a *taekbae* to pick up and deliver your luggage from the airport to your home. *Taekbae* is not able to process international deliveries, however.

The weight limit is usually 40 kg. If the package is over 30 kg or contains items of value, there may be additional fees. Items that are not deliverable include cash, checks, and anything valued at three million won (about $2,300 at the time of writing) or more. The post office, however, can deliver valuable items. If you record the total value of the package on the post office delivery form, they will automatically be insured. For added convenience, most couriers will contact you by phone a few minutes before arriving to check if you're ready to receive them.

PHRASES FOR DELIVERY SERVICES

I have a package for delivery.

○ 택배 좀 보내려고 하는데요.
taekbae jom bonaeryeogo haneundeyo.

What time can you pick it up?

○ 방문시간 좀 말씀해 주세요.
bangmunsigan jom malsseumhae juseyo.

When will it be delivered?

○ 언제쯤 물건이 도착하나요?
eonjejjeum mulgeoni dochakhanayo?

AT THE WORKPLACE

8 AT THE WORKPLACE

OVERVIEW Work Visas

Work Visas

If you are visiting the Republic of Korea for employment, for any business reason, or to teach English, you must get a work visa at a Republic of Korea embassy or consulate. If you enter the country and plan on staying for longer than 90 days, you will need to apply for an Alien Registration Card.

Work visas are usually valid for one year from the date of issue and take about two to four weeks for processing. Extensions are available if you remain with the same employer for longer. Visitors with work visas need to obtain a residence permit from the Immigration Office. Those engaged in earning activities without a work visa may be subject to fines and deportation.

Types of Employment Visa

Short-term employment (C-4)

Professorship (E-1)

Foreign language instructor (E-2)

Research (E-3)

Technology transfer (E-4)

Professional employment (E-5)

Arts & performances (E-6)

Special occupation (E-7)

Non-professional employment (E-9)

Vessel crew (E-10)

Working holiday (H-1)

Required Documents

*Passport

*Application for visa issuance

Other documents may be required, depending on the individual's circumstances. For detailed information according to visa type, please visit Korea's e-govermment website for foreigners: http://www.hikorea.go.kr/pt/index.html.

DAILY CONVERSATION IN THE OFFICE

water cooler talk

사무실 대화
samusil daehwa

Good morning!
○ 좋은 아침입니다!
jo-eun achimimnida!

How are you this morning?
○ 안녕하세요?
annyeonghaseyo?

Did you have a good weekend?
○ 주말 잘 쉬셨어요?
jumal jal swisyeosseoyo?

It's already lunchtime.
○ 벌써 점심시간이네요.
beolsseo jeomsimsiganineyo.

Let's go eat.
밥 먹으러 갑시다.
bap meogeureo gapsida.

Are you available for lunch?
점심시간에 시간 되세요?
jeomsimsigane sigan doeseyo?

What should we have for lunch today?
오늘은 뭘 먹으러 갈까요?
oneureun mwol meogeureo galkkayo?

Bon appetit. / Enjoy your meal.
잘 먹겠습니다.
jal meokgetseumnida.

I'm heading home now.
먼저 퇴근하겠습니다.
meonjeo toegeunhagetseumnida.

I will see you tomorrow.
내일 뵙겠습니다.
naeil boepgetseumnida.

I will see you next Monday.
다음 주 월요일에 뵙겠습니다.
da-eum ju woryoire boepgetseumnida.

Good-bye. (to person staying)
안녕히 계세요.
annyeonghi gyeseyo.

Goodbye. (to person leaving)

○ 안녕히 가세요.
annyeonghi gaseyo.

Have a nice evening!

○ 좋은 저녁 보내세요!
jo-eun jeonyeok bonaeseyo!

Have a nice weekend!

○ 좋은 주말 보내세요!
jo-eun jumal bonaeseyo!

OFFICE WORK

office

사무실
samusil

What's on your schedule today?

오늘 업무가 어떻게 되나요?
oneul eommuga eotteoke doenayo?

I will be working outside of the office today.

오늘 외근할 거예요.
oneul oegeunhal geoyeyo.

I don't have any appointments this morning.

오늘 오전에는 아무 약속도 없어요.
oneul ojeoneneun amu yaksokdo eopseoyo.

I will be in the office this afternoon.

오후에 사무실에 있을 거예요.
ohue samusire isseul geoyeyo.

I have something to take care of at the office this morning, and in the afternoon I have a meeting with a client.

○ 오늘 오전에는 사무실 업무를 보고, 오후에는 거래처와 미팅이 있어요.
oneul ojeoneneun samusil eommureul bogo, ohueneun georaecheowa miting-i isseoyo.

I have a general meeting at three o'clock today.

○ 오늘 오후 3시에 전체 회의가 있어요.
oneul ohu sesie jeonche hoe-uiga itseumnida.

Tonight we're having a team dinner.

○ 오늘밤 우리 팀 회식이 있어요.
oneulbam uri tim hoesigi isseoyo.

This morning I have a planning meeting, and I'm supposed to give a presentation on the report.

○ 오늘 오전에 기획회의가 있고, 제가 보고서를 발표할 예정이에요.
oneul ojeone gihoekhoe-uiga itgo, jega bogoseoreul balpyohal yejeong-ieyo.

Do you have a second?

○ 지금 시간 괜찮으세요?
jigeum sigan gwaenchaneuseyo?

I'm sorry, but I'm a little busy right now.

○ 죄송합니다만 지금 좀 바빠서요.
joesonghamnidaman jigeum jom bappaseoyo.

When are you free?

○ 언제 시간이 나나요?
eonje sigani nanayo?

---

presentation
프레젠테이션 / 발표
peurejenteisyeon / balpyo

How many slides are in the presentation?

○ 프레젠테이션이 몇 장이나 되나요?
peurejenteisyeoni myeot jang-ina doenayo?

Did you finish the presentation?

○ 프레젠테이션을 끝내셨어요?
peurejenteisyeoneul kkeunnaesyeosseoyo?

Can we schedule a meeting today?

○ 오늘 회의 좀 잡아주시겠어요?
oneul hoe-ui jom jabajusigesseoyo?

I need to check my e-mail.

○ 지금 이메일 체크해야 해요.
jigeum imeil chekeuhaeya haeyo.

Can you help me on this project?

이 프로젝트 하는 것 좀 도와주시겠어요?

peurojekteu haneun geot jom dowajusigesseoyo?

Can you forward that e-mail to me?

그 이메일 좀 나한테 포워드 시켜주시겠어요?

geu imeil jom nahante powodeu sikyeojusigesseoyo?

Can you send me the files that we discussed?

우리가 의논했던 파일 좀 보내주시겠어요?

uriga uinonhaetdeon pail jom bonaejusigesseoyo?

Did you get the e-mail I sent you?

내가 보낸 이메일 받았나요?

naega bonaen imeil badannayo?

Can you print six copies?

여섯 장만 복사해주시겠어요?

yeoseot jangman boksahaejusigesseoyo?

When are you getting your performance review this year?

올해 언제 업무평가를 받나요?

olhae eonje eommupyeongkkareul bannayo?

EXCUSES & APOLOGIES

being late

지각
jigak

I'm sorry I'm late.
○ 늦어서 죄송해요.
neujeoseo joesonghaeyo.

I had to go to the doctor.
○ 병원에 가야 했어요.
byeongwone gaya haesseoyo.

I missed my bus.
○ 버스를 놓쳤어요.
beoseureul nochyeosseoyo.

I overslept.
○ 늦잠 잤어요.
neutjam jasseoyo.

apologies

사과
sagwa

Something happened at home.

집에 급한 일이 생겨서요.
jibe geupan iri saenggyeoseoyo.

I took the wrong train.

지하철을 잘못 탔어요.
jihacheoreul jalmot tasseoyo.

Did you do it? / Is it done?

그거 했어요?
geugeo haesseoyo?

I thought it was due next week.

다음 주가 마감인줄 알았어요.
da-eum juga magaminjul arasseoyo.

Did you forget?

잊었어요?
ijeosseoyo?

I completely forgot about it.

○ 완전히 잊어버렸어요.
wanjeonhi ijeobeoryeosseoyo.

I'm really sorry.

○ 정말 미안해요.
jeongmal mianhaeyo.

The internet was down.

○ 인터넷이 끊겼어요.
inteonesi kkeunkyeosseoyo.

My computer crashed and I lost all the data.

○ 컴퓨터가 과부하 되어서 데이터가 다 날아갔어요.
keompyuteoga gwabuha doe-eoseo deiteoga da naragasseoyo.

I'm sorry. I will make sure this never happens again

○ 죄송합니다. 다음부터는 이런 일이 없도록 하겠습니다.
joesonghamnida. da-eumbuteoneun ireon ili eopdorok hagetseumnida.

I'll take extra care.

○ 특별히 주의하겠습니다.
teukbyeolhi juuihagetseumnida.

I won't be late again.

○ 다음부터는 시간을 꼭 지키겠습니다.
da-eumbuteoneun siganeul kkok jikigetseumnida.

OCCUPATIONS

occupation

직업
jigeobe

What do you do for a living?

○ 어떤 일을 하세요?
eotteon ireul haseyo?

I'm an English teacher.

○ 영어를 가르쳐요.
yeong-eoreul gareuchyeoyo.

I work for _____ (company).

○ 저는 _____에서 일합니다.
jeo-neun _____eseo ilhamnida.

I'm a computer programmer.

○ 저는 프로그래머입니다.
jeo-neun peurogeuraemeoimnida.

I'm a journalist.

◯ 저는 기자입니다.
jeo-neun gijaimnida.

Where is your office located?

◯ 사무실이 어디에요?
samusiri eodieyo?

My office is in _____ .

◯ 제 사무실은 _____에 있습니다.
je samusireun _____e itseumnida.

Are you satisfied with your job?

◯ 지금 직업에 만족하세요?
jigeum jigeobe manjokhaseyo?

Yes, I'm happy.

◯ 네, 만족해요.
ne, manjokhaeyo.

My work is interesting, but there's too much of it.

◯ 일은 재미있는데 너무 일이 많아요.
ireun jaemiinneunde neomu iri manayo.

OCCUPATIONS

english teacher

영어 선생님

yeong-eo seonsaengnim

businessperson

사업가 / 실업가

saeopga / sireopga

semiconductor engineer

반도체 엔지니어

bandoche enjinieo

computer programmer

프로그래머

peurogeuraemeo

judge

판사

pansa

lawyer

변호사

byeonhosa

cook

요리사

yorisa

professor

교수

gyosu

private academy instructor

학원 강사

hagwon gangsa

student

학생

haksaeng

doctor

의사

uisa

artist

예술가

yesulga

civil servant

공무원

gongmuwon

fashion designer

패션 디자이너

paesyeon dijaineo

SENIORITY

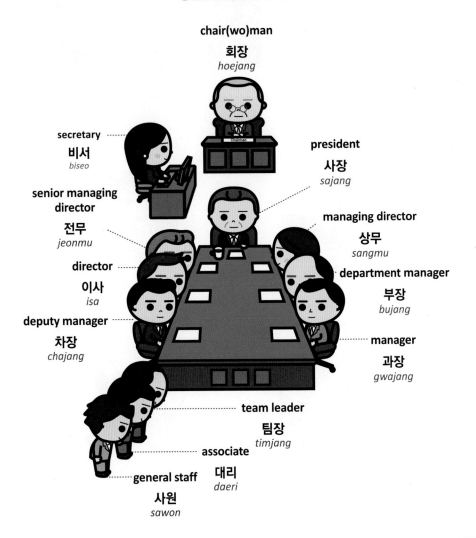

chair(wo)man
회장
hoejang

secretary
비서
biseo

president
사장
sajang

senior managing director
전무
jeonmu

managing director
상무
sangmu

director
이사
isa

department manager
부장
bujang

deputy manager
차장
chajang

manager
과장
gwajang

team leader
팀장
timjang

associate
대리
daeri

general staff
사원
sawon

DEPARTMENTS

human resources
인사부
insabu

quality control
품질관리부
pumjilgwallibu

administrative
경영관리부
gyeong-yeonggwallibu

design
디자인실
dijainsil

sales
영업부
yeong-eopbu

technical support
기술지원부
gisuljiwonbu

management
관리부
gwallibu

research
연구부
yeon-gubu

finances
재무부
jaemubu

general affairs
총무부
chongmubu

facilities
시설부
siseolbu

legal
법무부
beommubu

planning
기획부
gihoekbu

marketing
마케팅부
maketingbu

WEDDINGS & FUNERALS

groom
신랑
sillang

bride
신부
sinbu

tuxedo
턱시도
teoksido

wedding invitation
청첩장
cheongcheopjang

bouquet
부케
buke

wedding
결혼식
gyeolhonsik

Many traditions from Western weddings can also be found in Korea. It's very common to see a white dress on the bride and a black tuxedo on the groom, for example. Dedicated wedding halls and upscale hotel ballrooms are quick, efficient, and more commonly used than churches. These locations provide all the necessary services, including wedding dress and tuxedo rentals, photographers, and even catering. Don't be late: the ceremony and reception are often over in as little as 30 minutes.

Although guests usually bring presents to Western weddings, Korean guests give cash gifts instead. Coworkers, distant acquaintances, and friends of the parents come to congratulate the new couple and give cash gifts. Colleagues and close friends are generally expected to offer somewhere between 50,000 won and 100,000 won (US$45 to $90). Chaotic as it may seem, it's normal for several hundred people to show up.

photo of the deceased

영정사진
yeongjeongsajin

chief mourner

상주
sangju

funeral garment

상복
sangbok

wreath

화환
hwahwan

guest

조문객
jomun-gaek

incense

향
hyang

funeral

장례식
jangnyesik

Korean funerals traditionally last for three days before the burial. During the funeral, the body of the deceased is covered with a white sheet and placed behind a screen. In the viewing room, there is an altar with a photo of the deceased, a candle, and incense sticks.

Condolence money (*bujo*) is put in a white envelope, which you write your name on and place in a designated box. The Chinese characters 謹弔 (*geunjo*) translate to "sorry for your loss." The money goes to help pay the cost of the funeral.

Dressed in a black suit, the oldest son / chief mourner coordinates the events of the funeral. He stays in the viewing room, greeting guests and sitting on a coarse mat next to the photo of the deceased. After removing your shoes and entering the viewing room, you may notice a box of incense. Incense is thought to remove bad sprits and assist the

WEDDINGS & FUNERALS

deceased in reaching heaven. While standing or kneeling on the mat, light an incense stick with the burning candle and carefully place it in the urn.

If there is a vase of chrysanthemums and you don't want to bow, you should take one chrysanthemum and approach the photo on the altar in front of you. Place the chrysanthemum carefully on top of the others or on an empty space. Make sure that the stem is pointing toward you and that the flower faces the photo.

After departing the viewing room, put your shoes on and go to the food serving area. There, you'll find several main dishes, rice, kimchi, select fruits, beer, and soju.

how to perform a traditional bow
절 하는 법
jeol haneun beop

Approach the photo of the deceased while standing straight, right hand over left hand. Next, place both hands near eye level. Now, bend your waist and legs until your head, hands, and knees touch the floor. Perform two full bows as well as one from the waist before the photo. Finally, perform one full bow and one waist bow with the *sangju* (chief mourner).

EXPRESSING CONDOLENCES
TO THE CHIEF MOURNER AND FAMILY MEMBERS

Pray for the bliss of dead.

○ 고인의 명복을 빕니다.
goinui myeongbogeul bimnida.

Words can't express how sorry I am for your loss.

○ 어떻게 위로를 드려야 좋을지 모르겠습니다.
eotteoke wiroreul deuryeoya jo-eulji moreugesteumnida.

PLACES

9 PLACES

OVERVIEW Types of Places & Basic Expressions

general hospital
종합병원
jonghapbyeong-won

internal medicine
내과
naekkwa

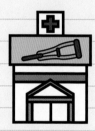

orthopedics
정형외과
jeonghyeong-oekkwa

dental clinic
치과
chikkwa

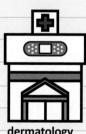

dermatology
피부과
pibukkwa

pediatrics
소아과
soakkwa

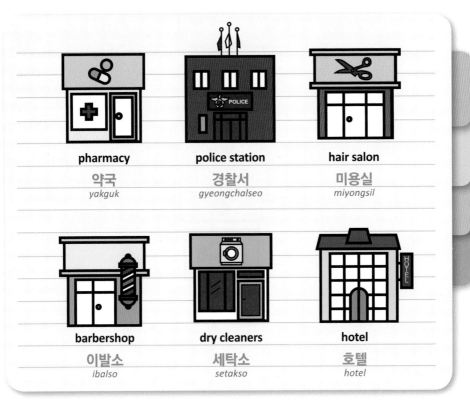

pharmacy
약국
yakguk

police station
경찰서
gyeongchalseo

hair salon
미용실
miyongsil

barbershop
이발소
ibalso

dry cleaners
세탁소
setakso

hotel
호텔
hotel

Is there a _____ around here?
근처에 _____가 / 이 어디 있나요?
geuncheo-e _____ga / i eodi innayo?

Can you recommend a good _____ (place)?
좋은 _____ 좀 알려주세요.
Jo-eun _____ jom allyeojuseyo.

Where's the nearest _____?
제일 가까운 _____은 / 는 어디죠?
jeil gakkaun _____eun / neun eodijyo?

hospital

병원
byeong-won

I'm sick.

아파요.
apayo.

Tell me where it hurts and how it feels.

어디가 어떻게 아픈지 말해 보세요.
eodiga eotteoke apeunji malhae boseyo.

I have a headache.

머리가 아파요.
meoriga apayo.

I'm dizzy.

머리가 어지러워요.
meoriga eojireowoyo.

I have chest pain.

⟳ 가슴이 아파요.
gaseumi apayo.

I'm having difficulty breathing.

⟳ 숨 쉬기가 곤란해요.
sum swigiga gollanhaeyo.

I have indigestion.

⟳ 소화가 안 돼요.
sohwaga an dwaeyo.

I'm nauseous. / I feel sick.

⟳ 속이 메스꺼워요.
sogi meseukkeowoyo.

I have heartburn.

⟳ 속이 쓰려요.
sogi sseuryeoyo.

I've been throwing up.

⟳ 구토를 해요.
gutoreul haeyo.

I have constipation.

⟳ 변비가 있어요.
byeonbiga isseoyo.

doctor

의사

uisa

I have diarrhea.

설사를 해요.
seolsareul haeyo.

I have a fever.

열이 나요.
yeori nayo.

I have been coughing and have a sore throat.

기침이 나고 목이 아파요.
gichimi nago mogi apayo.

I have a cold.

감기에 걸렸어요.
gamgie geollyeosseoyo.

I have the chills.

○ 오한이 나요.
ohani nayo.

My arm is swollen.

○ 팔이 부었어요.
pari bueosseoyo.

I accidentally cut myself.

○ 베였어요.
beyeosseoyo.

I can't stop bleeding.

○ 피가 안 멈춰요.
piga an meomchwoyo.

I burned my hand.

○ 손에 화상을 입었어요.
sone hwasang-eul ibeosseoyo.

I fell down.

○ 넘어졌어요.
neomeojyeosseoyo.

I sprained my ankle.

○ 발목을 삐었어요.
balmogeul ppieosseoyo.

I broke my leg.

○ 다리가 부러졌어요.
dariga bureojyeosseoyo.

symptom
증상
jeungsang

I'm allergic to _____.

○ _____에 알레르기가 있어요.
_____*e allereugiga isseoyo.*

I have insomnia.

○ 불면증이 있어요.
bulmyeonjjeung-i isseoyo.

I'm on my period.

○ 생리를 하는 중이에요.
saengnireul haneun jung-ieyo.

I have a toothache.

○ 이가 아파요.
iga apayo.

Recently, my teeth hurt.

○ 최근에 이가 시려요.
choegeune iga siryeoyo.

How long have you been sick?

언제부터 몸이 아팠습니까?
eonjebuteo momi apatseumnikka?

When did you first experience these symptoms?

언제부터 이런 증상이 있었죠?
eonjebuteo ireon jeungsang-i isseotjyo?

Please open your mouth wide.

입을 크게 벌리세요.
ibeul keuge beolliseyo.

Please take a deep breath.

숨을 크게 쉬어 보세요.
sumeul keuge swieo boseyo.

Lie down here, please.

여기에 누우세요.
yeogie nuuseyo.

Lie on your stomach, please.

배를 바닥에 붙이고 엎드리세요.
baereul badage buchigo eopdeuriseyo.

Please rinse out your mouth.

입을 헹구세요.
ibeul hengguseyo.

Have you had surgery before?

수술한 적이 있습니까?
susulhan jeogi itseumnikka?

There seems to be something wrong with my _____. I think I need to
have it checked out.

○ _____에 문제가 있는 것 같습니다. 정밀 검사를 해봐야겠습니다.

_____ e munjega inneun geot gatseumnida. jeongmil geomsareul haebwayagetseumnida.

What is your blood type?

○ 혈액형이 어떻게 되시죠?

hyeoraekhyeong-i eotteoke doesijyo?

My blood type is _____.

○ 제 혈액형은 _____형입니다.

je hyeoraekhyeong-eun _____ hyeong-imnida.

Roll up your sleeve for your shot.

○ 주사를 놓게 소매를 걷어 주세요.

jusareul noke somaereul geodeo juseyo.

Please come back in one week for another checkup.

○ 일주일 후에 다시 검사하러 오세요.

iljuil hue dasi geomsahareo oseyo.

Do you have medical insurance?

○ 보험이 있나요?

boheomi innayo?

pharmacy
약국
yakguk

pharmacist
약사
yaksa

I'd like to get this prescription filled.

◌ 이 처방전대로 약을 지어 주세요.
i cheobangjeondaero yageul jieo juseyo.

Do I need a prescription for this?

◌ 이 약은 처방전이 있어야 합니까?
i yageun cheobangjeoni isseoya hamnikka?

How often should I take this medicine?

◌ 이 약은 어떻게 복용합니까?
i yageun eotteoke bogyong hamnikka?

Take this medicine three times a day, 30 minutes after meals.

◌ 이 약은 하루 3번, 식후 30분에 복용하세요.
i yageun haru sebeon, sikhu samsipbune bogyonghaseyo.

POLICE STATIONS

police station

경찰서

gyeongchalseo

Where's the nearest police station?

가까운 경찰서가 어디죠?
gakkaun gyeongchalseoga eodijyo?

Help me!

도와주세요!
dowajuseyo!

How can I help you?

어떤 일로 오셨습니까?
eotteon illo osyeotseumnikka?

I've been robbed.

강도를 당했어요.
gangdoreul danghaesseoyo.

My ID card was stolen.

○ 제 신분증을 도둑맞았어요.
je sinbunjjeung-eul dodungmajasseoyo.

I lost my wallet / purse yesterday.

○ 어제 지갑을 잃어버렸어요.
eoje jigabeul ireobeoryeosseoyo.

I was attacked.

○ 폭행을 당했어요.
pokhaeng-eul danghaesseoyo.

I was overcharged.

○ 바가지 썼어요.
bagaji sseosseoyo.

Korea is a safe country to visit and live in. Drugs and weapons are illegal and very strictly controlled. The National Police Agency (NPA) is the name of the Korean police force (http://www.police.go.kr). And call 112 for the police.

You can find small police stations in every neighborhood. There are officers stationed there 24 hours a day. It's not uncommon to find police officers patrolling the streets, especially at night.

There are numerous security companies in Korea. SECOM is the largest, and their plaques are noticeable on many storefronts and office buildings. They, too, can be utilized for safety or security issues.

police officer
경찰관
gyeongchalgwan

I have been sexually molested.

성추행을 당했어요.
seongchuhaeng-eul danghaesseoyo.

My child is missing.

아이를 잃어버렸어요.
aireul ireobeoryeosseoyo.

Please help me find my child.

아이 찾는 걸 도와주세요.
ai channeun geol dowajuseyo.

I was in a car accident.

차 사고가 났어요.
cha sagoga nasseoyo.

I'm hurt.

○ 다쳤어요.
dachyeosseoyo.

I'm not hurt.

○ 안 다쳤어요.
an dachyeosseoyo.

I'm innocent.

○ 전 잘못이 없어요.
jeon jalmosi eopseoyo.

I need to contact my embassy.

○ 대사관에 연락하고 싶은데요.
daesagwane yeollakhago sipeundeyo.

I need an English-speaking lawyer.

○ 영어 하는 변호사를 불러주세요.
yeong-eo haneun byeonhosareul bulleojuseyo.

In other countries, it's common to find police hiding and ready to pounce on unsuspecting speedy drivers. However, those driving in Korea should beware of speed cameras instead. Thankfully, GPS devices will warn you to slow down as you approach these camera speed traps. Don't think you're off the hook just yet, though—speeding tickets can take up to a couple of months to arrive in your mailbox, catching you completely off guard.

Police set up random drunk driving checkpoints throughout Seoul. If your blood alcohol contentration is over 0.05 percent, you can lose your license, pay a hefty fine, and even go to prison. Drive responsibly.

HAIR SALONS & BARBERSHOPS

hair salon

미용실
miyongsil

barbershop

이발소
ibalso

How would you like your hair done?

○ 머리를 어떻게 하고 싶으세요?
meorireul eotteoke hago sipeuseyo?

I'd like to have my hair cut.

○ 머리를 자르고 싶어요.
meorireul jareugo sipeoyo.

How do you want your hair cut?

○ 머리를 어떻게 자르시겠어요?
meorireul eotteoke jareusigesseoyo?

Don't touch the top, please.

○ 윗머리는 깎지 마세요.
winmeorineun kkakji maseyo.

hair stylist

헤어 디자이너
he-eo dijaineo

Please leave my hairstyle the same and just take 2 cm off.

◌ 지금 헤어스타일 그대로 2센티미터만 잘라주세요.
jigeum he-eoseutail geudaero isentimiteoman jallajuseyo.

Please leave my bangs long.

◌ 앞머리를 길게 잘라주세요.
ammeorireul gilge jallajuseyo.

Please trim the ends.

◌ 머리끝만 다듬어주세요.
meorikkeunman dadeumeojuseyo.

Take some more off the sides.

◌ 양쪽 옆머리를 좀 더 잘라주세요.
yangjjok yeommeorireul jom deo jallajuseyo.

----

hairstyle

헤어스타일 / 머리모양
he-eoseutail / meorimoyang

I want my hair layered.

○ 머리에 층을 넣어주세요.
meorie cheung-eul neo-eojuseyo.

Can you make my hair look like this picture?

○ 제 머리를 이 사진이랑 똑같이 해주시겠어요?
je meorireul i sajinirang ttokgachi haejusigesseoyo?

Could you please trim my hair?

○ 머리 좀 다듬어 주시겠어요?
meori jom dadeumeo jusigesseoyo?

I'd like to get a perm.

○ 파마하고 싶어요.
pamahago sipeoyo.

Can you recommend a good hairstyle for me?

○ 저한테 어울릴 만한 헤어스타일 좀 추천해 주시겠어요?
jeohante eoullil manhan he-eoseutail jom chucheonhae jusigesseoyo?

Could you please dye my hair black?

머리를 검은색으로 염색해주세요.

meorireul geomeunsaegeuro yeomsaekhaejuseyo.

I want it thinned out.

머리숱 좀 쳐주세요.

meorisut jom chyeojuseyo.

A haircut and a shave, please.

이발하고 면도해 주세요.

ibalhago myeondohae juseyo.

Do you want your hair washed?

머리를 감겨 드릴까요?

meorireul gamgyeo deurilkkayo?

I want my hair blow-dried and styled.

드라이하고 스타일링도 해주세요.

deuraihago seutaillingdo haejuseyo.

Korea has barbershops for men and salons for women. Men can also choose to visit upscale salons for trendier hairstyles. Although it's not expected, tipping is becoming more common at salons and barbershops. If you like your new haircut and plan to visit the salon again, you may want to consider giving a small tip.

Appointments are not required unless you'd like to request a specific stylist. In that case, call ahead and make arrangements. Many salons open early and close after 10 pm to accomodate people's busy schedules.

dry cleaners

세탁소
setakso

What is the price for laundry services?

○ 세탁비가 얼마나 되나요?
setakbiga eolmana doenayo?

Can you remove the stain on this shirt?

○ 셔츠에 얼룩 좀 지워주시겠어요?
syeocheue eolluk jom jiwojusigesseoyo?

Do you offer same-day service?

○ 당일 세탁 서비스 가능한가요?
dang-il setak seobiseu ganeunghan-gayo?

Do you offer pickup or dropoff?

○ 배달도 해주나요?
baedaldo haejunayo?

Please be careful. The wool is delicate.

○ 이 울은 섬세하니까 조심해서 다뤄 주세요.
   i ureun seomsehanikka josimhaeseo darwo juseyo.

I'd like to get these clothes dry-cleaned.

○ 이 옷 드라이클리닝 해주세요.
   i ot deuraikeullining haejuseyo.

Do you do alterations?

○ 옷 수선도 가능한가요?
   ot suseondo ganeunghan-gayo?

About how long will the alterations take?

○ 고치려면 시간이 어느 정도나 걸리나요?
   gochiryeomyeon sigani eoneu jeongdona geollinayo?

Can you hem a pair of pants?

○ 바지 좀 줄여주시겠어요?
   baji jom juryeojusigesseoyo?

Can you replace this missing button?

○ 떨어진 단추 좀 달아주시겠어요?
   tteoreojin danchu jom darajusigesseoyo?

Can you sew this torn sleeve?

○ 찢어진 소매 좀 꿰매줄 수 있나요?
   jjijeojin somae jom kkwemaejul su innayo?

Can you replace a broken zipper?

○ 망가진 지퍼 좀 갈아주시겠어요?
   manggajin jipeo jom garajusigesseoyo?

delivery service

배달 서비스
baedal seobiseu

Can you take in the shoulder a bit?

○ 어깨 좀 줄여주시겠어요?
eokkae jom juryeojusigesseoyo?

This button is loose. Can you resew it?

○ 단추가 헐거운데, 다시 달아주시겠어요?
danchuga heolgeounde, dasi darajusigesseoyo?

It's too tight right here.

○ 여기가 너무 조여요.
yeogiga neomu joyeoyo.

It's too uneven there.

○ 거기가 너무 울퉁불퉁해요.
geogiga neomu ultungbultunghaeyo.

Can you fix this?

○ 고칠 수 있나요?
gochil su innayo?

Can you take in the body of a jacket?

◌ 재킷 품 좀 줄여주시겠어요?
jaekit pum jom juryeojusigesseoyo?

When will it be ready?

◌ 언제 되나요?
eonje doenayo?

In Korea, you'll find independent dry cleaners in every neighborhood. Many supermarket chains also offer laundry services. Chain stores may offer better pricing, since they handle higher volumes. Independent laundry shops offer specialized services such as stain treatment, basic alterations, and even delivery service. "Design reform" is the Korean phrase for making major alterations to clothing. If you need alterations like this, the area around Ewha Womans University in central Seoul has many shops that are known for quality clothing alterations at reasonable prices.

HOTELS

hotel

호텔

hotel

Good afternoon. Can I help you?

◌ 안녕하십니까? 무엇을 도와드릴까요?
annyeonghasimnikka? mueoseul dowadeurilkkayo?

I'd like to check in, please.

◌ 체크인 부탁드려요.
chekeuin butakdeuryeoyo.

Do you have a reservation?

◌ 예약은 하셨습니까?
yeyageun hasyeotseumnikka?

Yes, I have a reservation for two nights.

◌ 네, 이틀간 예약했습니다.
ne, iteulgan yeyakhaetseumnida.

reception

리셉션

resepsyeon

May I have your name?

○ 성함을 말씀해 주시겠습니까?
seonghameul malsseumhae jusigetseumnikka?

Do you have any rooms available tonight?

○ 오늘 묵을 방 있나요?
oneul mugeul bang innayo?

What kind of room do you have in mind?

○ 어떤 방을 원하십니까?
eotteon bang-eul wonhasimnikka?

I want a single room with a bath, please.

○ 욕실이 딸린 싱글 룸 부탁합니다.
yoksiri ttallin singgeul rum butakhamnida.

A single room is available tonight.

○ 네, 싱글 룸이 있습니다.
ne, singgeul rumi itseumnida.

How long are you planning to stay?

○ 얼마나 머무르실 계획입니까?
eolmana meomureusil gyehoegimnikka?

Just one night.

○ 하루만 숙박하겠습니다.
haruman sukbakhagetseumnida.

What is the room rate?

○ 방값이 얼마죠?
banggapsi eolmajyo?

A single is 70,000 won per night.

○ 싱글 룸은 하룻밤에 70,000원입니다.
singgeul rumeun harutbame chilmanwonimnida.

Is internet service included in the price?

○ 인터넷이 포함된 가격인가요?
inteonesi pohamdoen gagyeogin-gayo?

I would like a non-smoking room.

○ 비흡연실로 해주세요.
biheubyeonsillo haejuseyo.

Would you please register here? Also, could I please see your passport for a moment?

○ 숙박부에 기재해 주시겠습니까? 그리고 여권 좀 보여주세요.
sukbakbue gijaehae jusigesseumnikka? geurigo yeokkwon jom boyeojuseyo.

Of course. Here you are.

◌ 물론이죠. 여기 있습니다.
mullonijyo. yeogi itseumnida.

Here's your key card. Your room is No. 506. Have a pleasant stay.

◌ 여기 키 카드입니다. 고객님의 방은 506호입니다. 좋은 휴식 되십시오.
yeogi ki kadeuimnida. gogaengnimui bang-eun obaengnyukhoimnida. jo-eun hyusik doesipsio.

Hello, this is the front desk. How may I help you?

◌ 안녕하세요. 프런트입니다. 무엇을 도와드릴까요?
annyeonghaseyo. peureonteu-imnida. mueoseul dowadeurilkkayo?

This is Room 506. Could I have some extra pillows?

◌ 여기는 506호입니다. 베개를 좀 더 갖다 주시겠어요?
yeogineun obaengnyukhoimnida. begaereul jom deo gatda jusigesseoyo?

The _____ doesn't work.

◌ _____가 / 이 고장 났어요.
_____ ga / i gojang nasseoyo.

Can you please clean my room?

◌ 방 좀 청소해 주시겠어요?
bang jom cheongsohae jusigesseoyo?

PARTS OF THE BODY

body
몸
mom

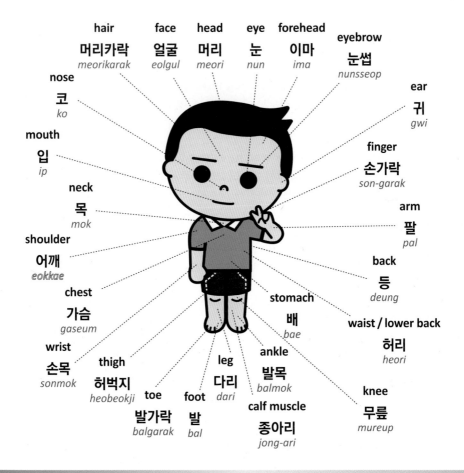

hair
머리카락
meorikarak

face
얼굴
eolgul

head
머리
meori

eye
눈
nun

forehead
이마
ima

eyebrow
눈썹
nunsseop

nose
코
ko

ear
귀
gwi

mouth
입
ip

finger
손가락
son-garak

neck
목
mok

arm
팔
pal

shoulder
어깨
eokkae

back
등
deung

chest
가슴
gaseum

stomach
배
bae

waist / lower back
허리
heori

wrist
손목
sonmok

thigh
허벅지
heobeokji

leg
다리
dari

ankle
발목
balmok

toe
발가락
balgarak

foot
발
bal

calf muscle
종아리
jong-ari

knee
무릎
mureup

My _____ hurts a bit.

_____를 좀 다쳤어요.

_____*reul jom dachyeosseoyo.*

My _____ hurts a lot.

_____가 너무 아파요.

_____*ga neomu apayo.*

tongue

혀

hyeo

teeth

이

i

muscle

근육

geunyuk

throat

목 / 목구멍

mok / mokgumeong

internal organs

체내 장기

chenae janggi

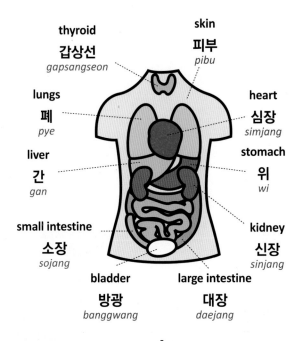

thyroid
갑상선
gapsangseon

skin
피부
pibu

lungs
폐
pye

heart
심장
simjang

liver
간
gan

stomach
위
wi

small intestine
소장
sojang

kidney
신장
sinjang

bladder
방광
banggwang

large intestine
대장
daejang

brain
뇌
noe

blood type
혈액형
hyeoraekhyeong

uterus
자궁
jagung

SYMPTOMS

symptoms
증상
jeungsang

headache
두통
dutong

dizziness
어지러움증
eojireoumjjeung

vomiting
구토
guto

burn
화상
hwasang

indigestion
소화불량
sohwabullyang

insect bite
벌레 물림
beolle mullim

fever
열
yeol

allergy
알레르기
allereugi

chills
오한
ohan

fracture
골절
goljjeol

to suffer a cut
베이다
beida

bleeding
출혈
chulhyeol

to sprain
삐다
ppida

TAKING MEDICINE

prescription
처방전
cheobangjeon

pain reliever
진통제
jintongje

ointment
연고
yeon-go

pill / tablet
알약
allyak

cold medicine
감기약
gamgiyak

sleeping pill
수면제
sumyeonje

liquid medicine

물약

muryak

Korean medicine

한약

hanyak

motion sickness pill

멀미약

meolmiyak

indigestion pill

소화제

sohwaje

diarrhea medicine

설사약

seolsayak

vitamins

비타민

bitamin

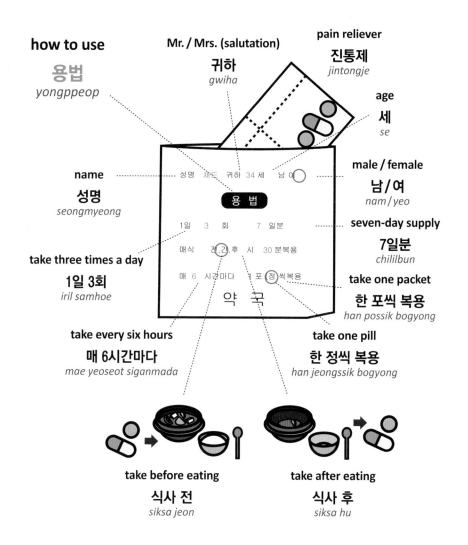

how to use
용법
yongppeop

Mr. / Mrs. (salutation)
귀하
gwiha

pain reliever
진통제
jintongje

age
세
se

name
성명
seongmyeong

male / female
남 / 여
nam / yeo

take three times a day
1일 3회
iril samhoe

seven-day supply
7일분
chililbun

take one packet
한 포씩 복용
han possik bogyong

take every six hours
매 6시간마다
mae yeoseot siganmada

take one pill
한 정씩 복용
han jeongssik bogyong

take before eating
식사 전
siksa jeon

take after eating
식사 후
siksa hu

용 법

성명   제도 귀하 34 세   남 여

1일   3   회   7 일분

매식   전 .2 . 후 시   30 분복용

매 6 시간마다   포 정 씩복용

약   국

HAIR SALONS & BARBERSHOPS

hair stylist
헤어 디자이너
he-eo dijaineo

blow-drying
드라이
deurai

mustache
콧수염
kotsuyeom

sideburns
구레나룻
gurenarut

root touchup
뿌리 염색
ppuri yeomsaek

beard
턱수염
teoksuyeom

shave
면도
myeondo

HAIRSTYLES

layered
레이어드
reieodeu

wavy
웨이브
weibeu

straight
스트레이트
seuteureiteu

bob
단발머리
danbalmeori

short
쇼트커트
syoteukeoteu

updo
올린머리
ollinmeori

bangs
앞머리
ammeori

haircut
커트
keoteu

FORTUNETELLERS

fortuneteller

무당 / 역술가
mudang / yeoksulga

At the beginning of the new year, people will often visit a fortune teller to see if they will enjoy good fortune in the coming months.

Young people use online fortunetellers that offer services for small fees. Older people, however, will spend at least 50,000 won per person visiting the fortune tellers in person. They take their fortunes more seriously than younger people and often make life-changing decisions based on the advice given to them.

There are two main types of fortunetellers in Korea. One is the shaman, also known as a *mudang*, and the second is a diviner (known as a *yeoksulga* or *yeoksurin*) who studies what are called the "Four Pillars." Each uses a different approach in foretelling the fate of their customer. The *mudang* acts as a medium for the spirits to share about the person's past life and future, speaking in the voice of a child or older person; some use rice to view the visitor's present and future. These fortunetellers will also use charms to ward off ill fortune. If they believe a person is being tormented by a particularly nasty spirit, they will perform an exorcism (called a *gut*) for a fee. The diviner, in contrast, studies the Chinese classics that explain the principles of the universe. Their determinations about a person's fate are based on the Four Pillars—the time, day, month, and year of their birth. They will ask the visitor for this information and select the appropriate fortune from their book, providing an account of that person's entire life.

Fortunetellers are also consulted on marriage compatibility and suitable baby names. Very few speak English, so those who'd like the experience of having their fortune told and finding out about their life are advised to visit with a friend who speaks Korean.

PHRASES FOR VISITING A FORTUNETELLER

I would like to ask you a question.
뭐 좀 물어보고 싶은데요.
mwo jom mureobogo sipeundeyo.

I would like to know about my fate (future).
제 운명(미래)에 대해 알고 싶습니다.
je unmyeong (mirae)-e daehae algo sipseumnida.

What is the time, day, month, and year of your birth?
생년월일시가 어떻게 되나요?
saengnyeonworilsiga eotteoke doenayo?

I was born at (time) on (month) (day), (year).
저는 년, 월, 일, 시에 태어났습니다.
jeo-neun (Y) nyeon, (M) wol, (d) il, (T) sie tae-eonasseumnida.

Do we make a good match?
이 사람과 궁합 좀 봐주시겠어요?
i saramgwa gunghap jom bwajusigesseoyo?

DRIVING

10 DRIVING

OVERVIEW Driver's License

Driving in Korea requires either a Korean or international driver's license. An international driver's license is issued in your home country and must be carried alongside your home country driver's license. It's typically valid for one year and can be renewed in your home country.

If you are a U.S. citizen, you may be able to exchange your home country driver's license for a Korean driver's license. You will need to pay a small fee and take a vision test. Later, when you're ready to leave Korea, you can show your airline ticket, passport, alien registration card, and Korean driver's license to have your home country license returned to you.

If you choose to apply for a Korean driver's license, you will need to pay a small fee, enroll in an one-hour traffic safety training class, take a forty-question multiple choice written test, take a driving course test, and perform a road test. The tests are available in English and other languages. They can all be taken on the same day, and are available on weekends.

In Korea, you must be 18 or older to drive a car, and at least 16 to drive a motorcycle. Driver's licenses are good for seven years. You can renew your license up to three months before expiration.

gas station

주유소
juyuso

Welcome!

어서 오세요!
eoseo oseyo!

How much is gas per liter?

리터당 얼마인가요?
riteodang eolmain-gayo?

Could you fill it up?

가득 채워주시겠어요?
gadeuk chaewojusigesseoyo?

Could you turn off the engine?

○ 엔진을 꺼주시겠어요?
enjineul kkeojusigesseoyo?

Could you open the gas cap?

○ 주입구를 열어주시겠어요?
juipgureul yeoreojusigesseoyo?

Can I have 50,000 won worth of regular unleaded?

○ 무연으로 50,000원어치만 넣어주시겠어요?
muyeoneuro omanwon-eochiman neo-eojusigesseoyo?

Which discount cards do you accept?

○ 어느 할인 카드를 받나요?
eoneu harin kadeureul batnayo?

I would like to have my car washed.

○ 외부 세차하고 싶은데요.
oebu sechahago sipeundeyo.

Korean vehicles run on several different fuels: LPG (liquid petroleum gas), diesel, and unleaded gasoline. If you have an LPG vehicle, look for an LPG fueling sign. However, there are far fewer LPG stations than unleaded and diesel ones. A GPS navigation system is the best way to locate these stations.

Certain credit cards and point cards may offer discounts on gas. The discount will be applied to your monthly statement, not on the gas receipt itself.

auto repair shop

자동차 정비소
jadongcha jeongbiso

Could you check my car for any problems?

○ 차에 문제가 있는지 점검 좀 해주시겠어요?
cha-e munjega inneunji jeomgeom jom haejusigesseoyo?

My car's been running loud lately.

○ 요즘에 제 차에서 소리가 나요.
yojeume je cha-eseo soriga nayo.

Could you check the muffler and exhaust system?

○ 머플러와 배기 장치를 점검 좀 해주시겠어요?
meopeulleowa baegi jangchireul jeomgeom jom haejusigesseoyo?

Could you test the brakes?

브레이크 좀 테스트해주시겠어요?
beureikeu jom teseuteuhaejusigesseoyo?

Can you recharge my air conditioner?

에어컨 가스 좀 넣어 주시겠어요?
e-eokeon gaseu jom neo-eo jusigesseoyo?

Can you replace the bulb in my headlight?

자동차 헤드라이트 전구 좀 갈아 주시겠어요?
jadongcha hedeuraiteu jeon-gu jom gara jusigesseoyo?

My car battery is dead.

차 배터리가 나갔어요.
cha baeteoriga nagasseoyo.

My car needs new tires.

새 타이어로 바꾸고 싶은데요.
sae taieoro bakkugo sipeundeyo.

Can you replace my radiator coolant?

라디에이터 냉각수 좀 보충해주시겠어요?
radieiteo naenggaksu jom bochunghaejusigesseoyo?

Could you put in some more wiper fluid?

윈도우액 좀 넣어 주시겠어요?
windouaek jom neo-eo jusigesseoyo?

Could you check the oil?

엔진 오일 좀 체크해주시겠어요?
enjin oil jom chekeuhaejusigesseoyo?

PARKING

public & valet parking

공공·& 대리 주차

gonggong & daeri jucha

Where can I park?

○ 어디다 주차를 해야 되나요?
eodida juchareul haeya doenayo?

How much does it cost to park?

○ 주차비가 얼마나 되죠?
juchabiga eolmana doejyo?

Restaurant customers have two hours of free parking.

○ 레스토랑 고객은 2시간까지 무료입니다.
reseutorang gogaegeun dusigankkaji muryoimnida.

How long can I park here?

○ 여기에 얼마나 오래 주차할 수 있죠?
yeogie eolmana orae juchahal su itjyo?

I'm sorry, but the parking lot is full.

◌ 죄송합니다만 주차장이 만차인데요.
joesonghamnidaman juchajang-i manchaindeyo.

Please be careful with my car.

◌ 제 차를 좀 조심해서 다뤄주세요.
je chareul jom josimhaeseo darwojuseyo.

Could you please validate my parking ticket?

◌ 여기에 도장 좀 찍어주시겠어요?
yeogie dojang jom jjigeojusigesseoyo?

My car has a scratch on it.

◌ 차가 긁혔어요.
chaga geulkyeosseoyo.

My car has a dent on it.

◌ 차가 찌그러졌어요.
chaga jjigeureojyeosseoyo.

I would like to get a monthly parking permit.

◌ 주차장 월 주차권을 구입하고 싶은데요.
juchajang wol juchakkwoneul gu-ipago sipeundeyo.

Many restaurants and shops offer valet parking. It's usually free, but may require a "tip" of a few thousand won.

Shopping centers and supermarkets normally offer discounted or free parking for their patrons. There may be a minimum purchase required to receive validated or discounted parking. Simply present your receipt as proof of payment to the attendant upon exiting the garage. Some parking areas require a validation stamp:

Churches, and doctor's offices are typical examples. Present the parking ticket at the parking garage front desk or to the business itself to obtain a stamp.

You may encounter automated parking garages that store your automobile in a large, secure car carousel. There's even a turntable to rotate your car in the correct direction.

Busy neighborhoods like Apgujeong-dong charge a premium for general parking. Be sure to check the rates before parking.

resident parking only

거주자 전용 주차공간

geojuja jeonyong juchagonggan

I'm here to visit my friend's apartment.

○ 이 아파트에 사는 친구를 방문하려고요.

i apateu-e saneun chin-gureul bangmunharyeogoyo.

What address are you going to?

○ 몇 동 몇 호 가세요?

myeot dong myeot ho gaseyo?

I'm visiting Apt. 302 in Block 408.

408동 302호에 왔어요.

sabaekpaldong sambaegiho-e wasseoyo.

How long will you be parking?

여기에 얼마나 오래 주차하실 건가요?

yeogie eolmana orae juchahasil geon-gayo?

Can you help me find a spot?

빈자리 찾는 것을 도와주시겠어요?

binjari channeun geoseul dowajusigesseoyo?

Can I park here?

여기 주차해도 되나요?

yeogi juchahaedo doenayo?

Please make sure your car is left in neutral.

기아를 중립으로 놓아 주세요.

giareul jungnibeuro noa juseyo.

Can you leave your car key here?

차 키를 여기에 맡겨 주시겠어요?

cha kireul yeogie matgyeo jusigesseoyo?

Can you please help me push these cars out of the way?

가로막은 차들을 미는 것을 도와주시겠어요?

garomageun chadeureul mineun geoseul dowajusigesseoyo?

This car is blocking me. Can you make an announcement to find the driver?

이 차가 제 차를 막고 있네요. 방송 좀 부탁드립니다.

i chaga je chareul makgo inneyo. bangsong jom butakdeurimnida.

Many older apartment complexes do not have enough spaces for their residents, let alone visitors. To create additional parking, cars can be placed perpendicularly in front of the parked cars. In case someone needs to push your car out of the way, make sure that your wheels are straight, the car is left in neutral, and the handbrake is disengaged. Also, post your cellphone number on the dashboard in case of an emergency.

If you're visiting someone's apartment, be sure to tell the security guard your plate number. Otherwise, you may find a difficult-to-remove warning sticker stuck to your windshield. When you're parked in a really tight space, it's best to leave your key with the security guard in case it needs to be moved.

Residential neighborhoods have prepaid street parking. But even for residents, these numbered spaces are hard to come by.

Be careful when choosing unmarked street parking spots. While it may seem like people leave their car wherever they feel, it's easy to get scratched, dented, or ticketed.

car accident
자동차 사고
jadongcha sago

Is this the police? There's been a car accident. Please come quickly.
경찰이죠? 여기 자동차 사고가 났어요. 빨리 와주세요.
gyeongcharijyo? yeogi jadongcha sagoga nasseoyo. ppalli wajuseyo.

I had a collision.
충돌이 일어났어요.
chungdori ireonasseoyo.

If you are involved in an auto accident, contact your insurance company from the accident scene. If an argument ensues between drivers, contact the police by dialing 112. And if someone is injured, call 119 and ask for an ambulance.

The insurance representatives will arrive and collect statements from both drivers. They will also examine the accident scene and take pictures of the vehicle damage. You will be notified by mail of the percentage of liability owed by each driver. It's uncommon for a driver to be deemed 100 percent liable for an accident.

I was driving when a pedestrian suddenly jumped in front of my car.

운전을 하고 있는데 보행자가 갑자기 뛰어 들었어요.

unjeoneul hago inneunde bohaengjaga gapjagi ttwieo deureosseoyo.

Is this 119? There's been an injury. Please hurry.

119죠? 여기 다친 사람이 있어요. 빨리 와주세요.

irilgujyo? yeogi dachin sarami isseoyo. ppalli wajuseyo.

How can I help you?

어떻게 도와드릴까요?

eotteoke dowadeurilkkayo?

I was just in a car accident.

자동차 사고가 났어요.

jadongcha sagoga nasseoyo.

Can you send someone over?

사람 좀 보내주시겠어요?

saram jom bonaejusigesseoyo?

Was anyone injured?

다치신 분이 있나요?

dachisin buni innayo?

No, we are all okay.

아니요, 다 괜찮아요.

aniyo, da gwaenchanayo.

injury

부상
busang

Yes, someone was hurt.

○ 네, 다친 사람이 있어요.
ne, dachin sarami isseoyo.

- -

Did you call 119?

○ 119에는 연락하셨습니까?
irilgu-eneun yeollakhasyeosseumnikka?

- -

Yes, I did.

○ 네, 연락했어요.
ne, yeollakhaesseoyo.

- -

No, not yet.

○ 아니오. 아직이요.
anio. ajigiyo.

- -

If this is an emergency, please call 119 and an ambulance.

○ 응급 처치가 필요하시면, 119에 전화해서 구급차를 부르세요.
eunggeup cheochiga piryohasimyeon, irilgu-e jeonhwahaeseo gugeupchareul bureuseyo.

- -

Can you explain what happened?

○ 사고 정황을 말씀해 주실 수 있나요?
sago jeonghwang-eul malsseumhae jusil su innayo?

We had a minor accident / fender-bender.

○ 접촉사고가 났어요.
jeopchoksagoga nasseoyo.

The front end of the car was damaged.

○ 차 앞 쪽이 부서졌어요.
cha ap jjogi buseojyeosseoyo.

Someone will be there shortly to collect information and assist you.

○ 사고 처리를 도와드릴 직원을 빨리 보내 드리겠습니다.
sago cheorireul dowadeuril jigwoneul ppalli bonaedeurigetseumnida.

ROAD

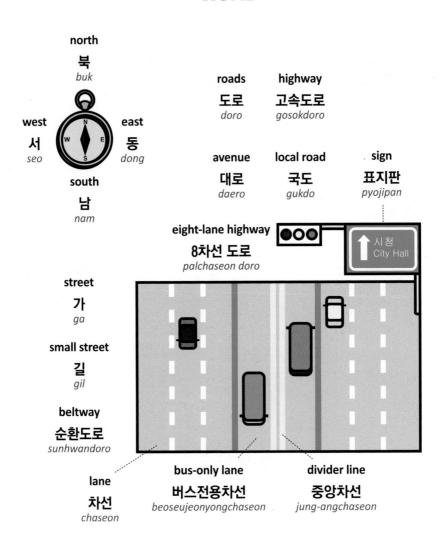

north
북
buk

west
서
seo

east
동
dong

south
남
nam

roads
도로
doro

highway
고속도로
gosokdoro

avenue
대로
daero

local road
국도
gukdo

sign
표지판
pyojipan

eight-lane highway
8차선 도로
palchaseon doro

시청
City Hall

street
가
ga

small street
길
gil

beltway
순환도로
sunhwandoro

lane
차선
chaseon

bus-only lane
버스전용차선
beoseujeonyongchaseon

divider line
중앙차선
jung-angchaseon

CAR PARTS

turn signal
방향 지시등 / 깜박이
banghyang jisideung / kkambagi

hood
본네트
bonneteu

roof
루프
rupeu

trunk
트렁크
teureongkeu

bumper
범퍼
beompeo

tire
타이어
taieo

steering wheel
운전대
unjeondae

seat
좌석
jwaseok

ignition
시동 스위치
sidong seuwitch

car key
차 열쇠
cha yeolsoe

windshield wipers
유리 와이퍼
yuri waipeo

vent
통풍구
tongpunggu

dashboard
계기판
gyegipan

gear shift
기어
gieo

brake pedal
브레이크
beureikeu

gas pedal
액셀러레이터
aekselleoreiteo

glove compartment
조수석 도구함
josuseok doguham

GAS STATION

gas station

주유소

juyuso

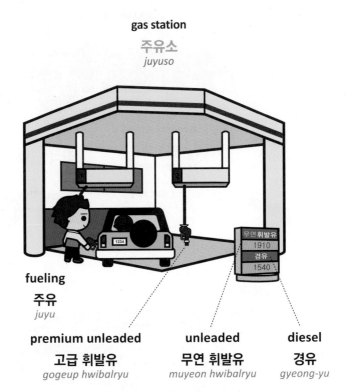

fueling

주유

juyu

premium unleaded

고급 휘발유

gogeup hwibalryu

unleaded

무연 휘발유

muyeon hwibalryu

diesel

경유

gyeong-yu

AUTO REPAIR SHOP

auto repair shop
자동차 정비소
jadongcha jeongbiso

tow truck
견인차
gyeonincha

PUBLIC & VALET PARKING

parking ticket
주차증
juchajeung

validation stamp
주차 도장
jucha dojang

32가 1256

license plate number
차 번호판
cha beonhopan

parking garage
주차장
juchajang

monthly parking permit
월 주차권
wol juchakkwon

RESIDENT PARKING ONLY

PERMIT REQUIRED

resident parking only
거주자 전용 주차공간
geojuja jeonyong juchagonggan

handicapped parking
장애인 주차구역
jang-aein juchaguyeok

no parking
주차금지
juchageumji

공영 주차장

P

public parking
공영 주차장
gong-yeong juchajang

OUT **P** IN

underground parking
지하 주차장
jiha juchajang

PASSENGER SEATING
& STREET PARKING

passenger seating

차의 상석 문화
cha-ui sangseonkmunhwa

If there's a *sajang* or a passenger
older than driver in the car

In the West, the seat next to the driver is is most desirable. But in Korea, the best seat for an important or older passenger is thought to be the one in the back at a diagonal from the driver's seat—i.e., the most convenient one for getting in and out. It's known as the "sajang's seat," after the word for a company president, and you can earn some points by offering it to a valued business guest or someone you wish to impress.

Oddly enough, the "shotgun" seat is typically viewed as the place for someone to assist the driver: preparing snacks on long trips or looking out for road signs and directions. Obviously, this isn't an issue between close friends.

street parking

노면주차
nomyeonjucha

Seoul, and Korea in general, is home to a lot of cars and relatively few parking spaces. Finding downtown parking is often a tall order. Often times, visitors to commercial areas, smaller stores, and restaurants or shops with a longstanding reputation will find there is nowhere to park. When this happens, don't go circling around in search of a spot. Instead, step inside the establishment and ask someone where you can park. Typically, they tell you where the parking lot is located. Or many tell you to park on the road in front. But you have to be careful, for these days parking enforcement vehicles with cameras can snap a photo and fine you.

APPENDIX >>>>>>

NUMBERS

Pure Korean numbers		Sino-Korean numbers	
One 하나 *hana* 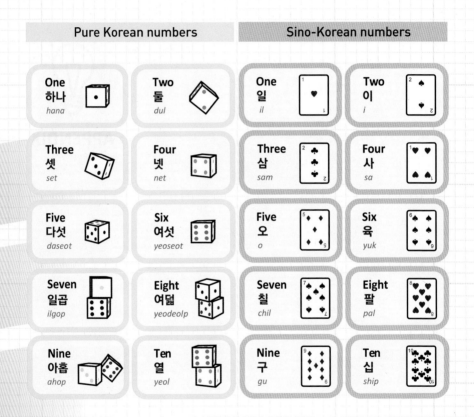	**Two** 둘 *dul*	**One** 일 *il*	**Two** 이 *i*
Three 셋 *set*	**Four** 넷 *net*	**Three** 삼 *sam*	**Four** 사 *sa*
Five 다섯 *daseot*	**Six** 여섯 *yeoseot*	**Five** 오 *o*	**Six** 육 *yuk*
Seven 일곱 *ilgop*	**Eight** 여덟 *yeodeolp*	**Seven** 칠 *chil*	**Eight** 팔 *pal*
Nine 아홉 *ahop*	**Ten** 열 *yeol*	**Nine** 구 *gu*	**Ten** 십 *ship*

The Korean language uses two sets of numbers. Anything that can be counted will require use of only one of these sets. Pure Korean numbers are of Korean origin. Sino-Korean numbers derive from Chinese.

Ordinal numbers

First
첫 번째
cheot beonjjae

Second
두 번째
du beonjjae

Third
세 번째
se beonjjae

Fourth
네 번째
ne beonjjae

Fifth
다섯 번째
daseot beonjjae

Sixth
여섯 번째
yeoseot beonjjae

Seventh
일곱 번째
ilgop beonjjae

Eighth
여덟 번째
yeodeol beonjjae

Ninth
아홉 번째
ahop beonjjae

Tenth
열 번째
yeol beonjjae

Eleventh
열한 번째
yeolhan beonjjae

Zero
영, 공
yeong, gong

Hundred
백
baek

Thousand
천
cheon

Ten thousand
만
man

Hundred thousand
십만
shipman

Million
백만
baekman

Pure Korean numbers are only commonly used to represent 1 to 99. Ordinal numbers are a variation of this. The yellow boxes are ordinals of pure Korean numbers showing ranking. The below column is a set of Sino-Korean numbers are used with large numbers, such as money.

Author	Chad Meyer
Illustration	Kim Moon-jung
Publisher	Kim Hyung-geun
Editor	Jang Woo-jung
Copy Editor	Daisy Larios, Colin Mouat
Designer	Lee Bok-hyun